W.G.B.

S. U. from A. C.
"Jolly Days"
1941.

THE CHARM OF CAMBRIDGE

KING'S COLLEGE CHAPEL: INTERIOR

THE CHARM OF CAMBRIDGE

WRITTEN BY

S. C. ROBERTS

Fellow of Pembroke College

ILLUSTRATED BY

W. G. BLACKALL

A. & C. BLACK, LTD.

4, 5 & 6 SOHO SQUARE, LONDON, W.1

1933

Printed in Great Britain
First Edition published November, 1927
Second Edition April, 1933

PREFACE

IN his preface to *The Charm of Oxford*, a title which has pre-determined that of the present volume, Dr Wells declares that his justification lies in Mr Blackall's drawings.

For the compilation of this book I must plead a similar excuse. Books on Cambridge abound, and my own slight sketches of college history are in no way intended to compete with the work of the social and architectural historians—Gunning, Cooper, Willis and Clark, and many others—to whom, indeed, my debt is obvious. I have rather endeavoured, with the help of Mr Blackall's drawings and with the minimum of historical and architectural detail, to guide the reader through those buildings of which Charles Lamb said that he "could live and die in them and never wish to speak again."

S. C. R.

September 1927.

NOTE

I have taken the opportunity afforded by a second edition of making a number of small corrections and additions. These are mainly due to the rapid growth of university and college buildings in the last six years.

February, 1933

S. C. R.

CONTENTS

LIST OF ILLUSTRATIONS

LIST OF ILLUSTRATIONS

THE APPROACH TO CAMBRIDGE

THE APPROACH TO CAMBRIDGE

IF it be true that first impressions are important, the traveller should approach Cambridge by road, and preferably by the London road, which will bring him past the old toll-house through Trumpington, Chaucer's Trumpington, whose church can boast of one of the best known brasses in England, and whose war memorial displays a most surprising modernity of design. From Trumpington, a truly spacious English road, lined with elms in which nightingales still sing, leads to the edge of the town itself. Here a milestone marks " One mile to Great St Mary's." It is no ordinary milestone. It bears the arms of Trinity Hall, in commemoration of Dr Mowse, Master of that college, who left money to pay for the repair of the highways round Cambridge. The sixteen milestones along the lonely road to Barkway were set up early in the eighteenth century and are said to be the first erected in England since Roman times.

Immediately on the left is a triangle of common land which marks the beginning of the Fen country. It is in fact a corner of Coe (or Cow) Fen, where in the eighteenth century Henry Gunning and his friends used to go for snipe-shooting, and where now the Leys School and the Engineering Laboratory frown at each other across what was formerly Coe Fen Lane. Now, however, both the lane and its title have been enlarged and the Fen Causeway leads down to the latest of the Cam bridges.

By this time the traveller is at the corner of Lensfield Road, round which the taxi-cabs come swirling from the station into Trumpington Street proper. Trumpington Street has no single sweeping curve ; nor has it any carefully-ordered series of collegiate buildings. But it is one of the most surprising streets in England. In its first curve stand terraces of solid nineteenth-century houses, many of them representing the earliest refuge and stronghold of the married don ; others have long since been transformed into undergraduate lodging-houses. On the right stands Addenbrooke's Hospital, girt, as Mr E. M. Forster says, like any Venetian palace with a mantling canal. Streams, indeed, run along each side of the street, relics of a complicated system of waterways introduced into Cambridge in the seventeenth century. The parent stream rises in the springs near Great Shelford, called " Nine Wells," and was diverted at the suggestion of Andrew Perne, Master of Peterhouse, in 1610. Popular tradition, however, knows nothing of Perne in this matter ; and the conduit will for all time be associated with Thomas Hobson, the university carrier immortalised both in Milton's epitaph and in *The Spectator*.

" Mr *Hobson*," wrote Steele, " kept a Stable of forty good Cattle, always ready and fit for travelling ; but when a Man came for a Horse, he was led into the Stable, where there was great Choice, but he oblig'd him to take the Horse which stood next to the Stable-door ; so that every Customer was alike well-serv'd according to his Chance, and every Horse ridden with the same Justice : From whence it became a Proverb, when what ought to be your Election was forc'd upon you, to say, *Hobson's Choice*."

Originally " Hobson's Conduit " stood on Market Hill ; but since 1855 it has stood proudly at the end of Brookside with its inscription freshly painted for every incoming visitor to see.

Opposite Addenbrooke's stands the Fitzwilliam Museum, the art treasury of the University, which has grown out of a bequest made by Viscount Fitzwilliam in 1810. It is one of the finest classical buildings in Cambridge and is a fitting memorial of its architect, Basevi, who, before the completion of the Museum, was killed by a fall from some scaffolding in Ely Cathedral. In recent years a bequest of exceptional munificence has come to the Fitzwilliam under the will of the late Charles Brinsley Marlay, of Trinity College. To accommodate the Marlay and other collections new wings (one of them due to the generosity of the Courtauld family) were completed in 1931. The Museum makes an appeal to a circle far wider than that of the professed connoisseur. Amongst the manuscripts, for instance, the mediævalist may contemplate the superb Metz Pontifical, the most beautiful French liturgical manuscript of the early fourteenth century ; the lover of eighteenth-century *Realien* may prefer to study the ledgers of Sir Joshua Reynolds ; the enthusiast for modern writers may read *The Psalm of Montreal* or *Grantchester* in its original script. Similarly amongst the pictures the visitor may wander from Rembrandt's *Man with Plumed Hat* to Gainsborough's portrait of the Hon. W. Fitzwilliam, or to Raeburn's portrait of W. Glendouwyn, or to Hogarth's *A Musical Party* ; and from Hogarth to Turner and the Pre-Raphaelites ; and from the Pre-Raphaelites to William Nicholson and Augustus John and Max Beerbohm. Lastly, from a certain window, which looks northwards across the garden of Peterhouse, something may be learnt of the unexpected charm of Cambridge.

The name of Fitzwilliam is further commemorated in a house and in a street. Fitzwilliam Street is now little more than two rows of lodging-houses, but amongst its lodgers have been Charles Darwin and Charles Kingsley. Fitzwilliam

House, a good Georgian building, is the headquarters of the non-collegiate students, and bears its date (1727) just above one of the ground-floor windows.

It is fitting that the first college that the traveller sees —Peterhouse—should be the oldest. But the university is older than the colleges, and the town of Cambridge is older than both. Early in the twelfth century the canons of St Giles had established themselves in a new Priory at Barnwell; on the site of St John's College was the Augustinian Hospital of St John; and on the site of Jesus College was the Nunnery of St Radegund. A body of Franciscans settled in Cambridge in 1224, and early in the thirteenth century a number of " clerks " came over from Oxford. While seniority of origin must certainly be conceded to the sister university, the migration of 1209 may fairly be taken as evidence that schools were in existence at Cambridge before that date. In any event, the thirteenth-century student was essentially a wanderer, and a riot in Oxford would result in a migration to Cambridge and *vice versa*. The students, following continental practice, grouped themselves according to nationality. The Trent was approximately the dividing-line, and North and South (the latter including the Irish and Welsh) waged great battles. Thus in 1261 the Northerners were defeated and seceded in considerable numbers to Northampton. There they combined with some Oxford seceders to found a university at Northampton. A royal mandate was obtained for a new *studium generale*, but three years later the foundation was dissolved. Besides these academic factions, " Town and Gown " riots were a prominent feature of mediæval Cambridge. In origin they were probably not very different from the troubles of later centuries. A scholar would be committed to prison for some misdemeanour; his fellows would quickly organise a rescue-party which would be resisted by the towns-men ; a counter-attack would be made upon the students' hostel and the upshot would be plunder, fire, and destruction. " Strifes, fights, spoilings, breaking open of houses, wound-ings and murder betwixt the burgesses and the scholars of Cambridge," wrote Matthew Paris, " and that in the very Lent, that, with the holy time holy persons also might be violated. The noise thereof ascended to the ears of the King with a great complaint."

But of course the thirteenth-century student did not spend his whole time in " ragging." He entered the University at the age of fourteen, or even younger, having little know-ledge except of the rudiments of Latin. If his Latin was weak, he was given instruction in grammar, but normally he went through a course of Logic in his first year, at the end of which he was called upon to prove his worth in a disputation. Next he studied Rhetoric, a Latin translation of Aristotle's treatise being his principal text. Having com-pleted this threefold course of study, or *trivium*, and having satisfactorily performed his disputations in the schools as a sophister or disputant, the student became an " incepting " bachelor, which may originally have meant that he was now an apprentice to a Master, under whom he would proceed to the further fourfold course (or *quadrivium*) of arithmetic, geometry, music, and astronomy. At the end of the four years occupied by this course, the student was eligible to be admitted to the degree of Master of Arts and to begin to give lectures himself. Such lectures were given either in a hired house, or in the precincts of one of the great religious foundations, or even in a church. The student lived in a hostel under the direction of a Master or in lodgings hired from a townsman. As early as 1231, student-life was a sufficiently important feature of Cambridge to cause King

Henry III to issue a series of writs. By one of these the Sheriff was empowered to punish insolent clerks and scholars with the approval of the Bishop and of the Chancellor and Masters of the University; by another, those clerks who were not under the tuition of a Master were forbidden to remain in the University; by another, the rents of lodgings were ordered to be controlled by two Masters and two " good and lawful men of the town." These mandates illustrate the difficulties of supervision and control with which the Town and the University were faced, and it was not until the foundation of the colleges that the University was able to exercise a proper discipline over its members.

Hugh de Balsham, Bishop of Ely from 1257 to 1286, a far-seeing and liberal-minded prelate, took up the cause of the education of the ordinary priest as opposed to that of the religious orders. With this object in view, he first attempted in 1281 to introduce a number of secular scholars into the dwelling-place of the secular brethren of the Hospital of St John. But the two elements did not combine happily, and the Bishop moved his scholars to the other end of the town, the Augustinians giving to them St Peter's Church (on the site of which St Mary the Less now stands) and two neighbouring hostels.

Thus the first Cambridge college came into being.

PETERHOUSE: THE OLD COURT AND CHAPEL

PETERHOUSE

PETERHOUSE

O N 28th May 1284, the " studious scholars " of Hugh
de Balsham " who should in everything live
together as students in the University of Cambridge
according to the rule of the Scholars at Oxford who are called
of Merton," were by Royal Charter confirmed in the possession of their *Domus Sancti Petri, sive Aula scholarium
Episcopi Eliensis*.

When Hugh de Balsham died in 1286, he left 300 marks
to his scholars, and with this they bought " a certain area
to the south of the Church, and built thereon a handsome
Hall." Little of the fabric of this hall remains, but on the
extreme right of the picture there may just be seen the
buttresses which mark the entrance doorways. These doorways, on each side, are original and are thus the oldest relics
of collegiate building in Cambridge. The oriel window of
the hall was the work of Sir Gilbert Scott, but on the south
side the fifteenth-century windows remain, and there now
belongs to them the added glory of stained glass windows
designed by William Morris. The Combination Room, formed
out of the old Stone Parlour built in 1460 and the Inner
Parlour of 1595, boasts of similar glass, and is one of the
loveliest rooms in Cambridge. St Peter's Church and, after
its destruction, St Mary the Less, built between 1340 and
1352, served the college for chapel until 1632. Of Little
St Mary's it may be noted that its decorated east window is

one of outstanding beauty. Like many of the beauties of Cambridge, it is partially hidden.

The chapel of Peterhouse, standing uniquely in the middle of the court, was consecrated by Matthew Wren (Master of the College, Bishop of Ely, and uncle of Sir Christopher) in 1632. Wren and his successor, Cosin, belonged to the party of Archbishop Laud and their chapel, with its mediæval tracery without and its High Church ritual within, became a prominent target for Puritan attack.

"In Peter House Chappel," wrote Prynne, "there was a glorious new Altar set up, and mounted on steps, to which the Master, Fellows, Schollers bowed . . . and on the Altar a Pot, which they usually called the incense pot . . . and the common report both among the Schollers of that House and others, was, that none might approach to the Altar in Peterhouse but in Sandalls."

Galleries, built over arcades, connected the chapel with the buildings on either side of the court, the one on the south leading to what was once the Master's Lodge. But Peterhouse, like several other colleges, has been obliged to drive its Master *extra portas*. The Master was originally lodged in the building above the present Combination Room, and when Andrew Perne died in 1589 and left his books to the college, he laid down in his will that he wished the " Colledge Librairie to be newe builded at the east end of the Masters Lodginge longewayes towardes the Streate."

Accordingly a library was built on the ground floor, and above it a long narrow room, or gallery, for the Master. Such a room was a common feature of country houses and master's lodges in the sixteenth century, and at Queens', the President's Lodge may be seen in its original splendour. At Peterhouse the old Lodge was used as such until the beginning of the eighteenth century, but in 1725 Dr Charles Beaumont, son of the Master, bequeathed to the college his own noble house on the other side of Trumpington Street. Here, in suitable dignity, the Masters of Peterhouse have continued to live, and in 1927 there was completed alongside of it a new block of college buildings, the beginnings of what may eventually be a new court.

But the charm of Peterhouse is not wholly contained in its buildings. Behind the main court is Gisborne Court, built in 1826, and a gate in the far corner leads to a deer park, the only one in Cambridge and the smallest in England. There are few better resting-places than this famous Grove. The wall which divides it from the fen has stood for more than 400 years.

Of the early Masters of Peterhouse the most notable was Andrew Perne. A benefactor both to his college and to the University, Perne displayed a remarkable elasticity of religious opinion. He was in high favour with Edward VI, and was equally successful in the reign of Mary, being appointed Dean of Ely as well as Master of Peterhouse. In the next reign he remained in office and preached before the Queen in King's College Chapel in 1564. It is not surprising that the verb *pernare* was coined to mean " to be a turn-coat," and that the letters A.P.P. on the college weather-vane were held to stand for " Andrew Perne, Papist," or " Andrew Perne, Protestant," according to the direction of the theological winds.

With a later Master a famous anecdote is associated. Francis Barnes, Master from 1788 to 1838, was Vice-Chancellor when the Knightbridge Professorship of Moral Philosophy was vacant. The electors were the Vice-Chancellor, two Professors of Divinity, and the Master of Peterhouse. Barnes, as Vice-Chancellor, nominated himself for the vacancy; as Master of Peterhouse, he seconded the nomination; when the other electors nominated another candidate, Barnes, as chairman, gave his casting vote in favour of himself. The details of the story do not bear the test of research into the relevant dates. But it is a story that deserves to be "emancipated from the bonds of fact."

A yet more famous Peterhouse anecdote is that concerning Thomas Gray. Gray first entered the college in 1734 and returned to it in 1742. In January 1756 he wrote to Wharton asking him to buy a rope-ladder, "full 36 Foot long," which should have "strong hooks . . . to throw over an Iron bar to be fixed withinside of my window." Certainly the bar was fixed, though not inside the window, and there it remains for tourists to see to-day. The popular version of the story of what followed is that two noisy fellow-commoners, having raised a false alarm of fire and placed a tub of water beneath the poet's window, had the satisfaction of seeing him slide down the rope into the water. For the water-tub there is no authority, but for the rest of the story there is good documentary evidence; on 6th March 1756 Gray migrated to Pembroke where he was "extremely well-lodged" and "as quiet as in the Grande Chartreuse."

In modern times Peterhouse, the college of Henry Cavendish, has been the home of some of the great physicists of the nineteenth century—Kelvin, Tait, and Dewar; and it is fitting that, as a result of Lord Kelvin's enthusiasm, Peterhouse should have been the first Cambridge college to be lighted throughout by electric light.

In the sphere of the humanities the most distinguished Peterhouse figure in recent years was that of Sir Adolphus William Ward. Elected to the mastership at the age of sixty-two at the beginning of the century, he worked for the College and the University with amazing vigour right up to the time of his death in 1924. More recently Peterhouse has made history by choosing a Field-Marshal as its Master.

PEMBROKE COLLEGE

PEMBROKE COLLEGE, FROM TRUMPINGTON STREET

CROSSING the road, like Gray, we come to Pembroke. *O domus antiqua et religiosa*, Queen Elizabeth is said to have exclaimed as she passed its gate in 1566. Ancient and religious indeed was the foundation of what was originally known as the Hall of Valence Mary.

Mary de Saint Paul, daughter of Guy de Chastillion, and the second wife of Aymer de Valence, Earl of Pembroke, became early a widow. The common legend, indeed, is that, " her husband being unhappily slain at a tilting at her nuptials," she was maid, wife, and widow all in a day. The legend, though immortalised by Gray :

> And sad *Chatillon*, on her bridal morn
> That wept her bleeding Love

is now discredited, but about the benefactions of Lady Mary de Valence there can be no controversy. Retiring from the world herself, she endowed a nunnery of Minoresses at Waterbeach, and transferred it to Denny Abbey, to be governed " according to the strict and famous order of St Clare "; she also secured a site for a college in Cambridge just outside the gates of the mediæval town. The foundation of the college was to consist of a Master, twenty-four Fellows, and six Scholars ; " and it was enjoined on those who were elected into her college to be constant in their visits to this religious

3

house [Denny Abbey], as their ghostly counsellors and instructors."

Denny Abbey has all but vanished, but Pembroke Hall, as it soon came to be called, has immensely outgrown its Foundress's original plan. Yet, until about fifty years ago most of the original buildings remained. These buildings were contained in a tiny court about half the size of the present Old Court, and consisted of a chapel on the north side, a kitchen and buttery in the north-east corner, a hall on the east side with a combination room and master's lodgings, and chambers on the south and west sides. Here were "all the component parts of a complete collegiate establishment" surviving, with certain modifications, until 1874, when, by a narrow majority, the Fellows decided to pull down the old Hall, the old Master's lodge, and the range of chambers on the south side of the court.

> A Quaker saint, as architect call'd in
> Hall, library, and half the house—just Heaven !
> From the foundations Mary laid did blast.
> What is the punishment when good men sin ?

Of course, there had been architectural changes, though of a less sweeping kind, before 1874. Pembroke was the first college to have its own chapel. Originally the scholars used the neighbouring church of St Botolph, but in 1355 the Foundress obtained a licence from Pope Urban V to build a chapel within the college walls. This chapel served for three hundred years. In 1659, Matthew Wren, Bishop of Ely, whom we have already met at Peterhouse, was released from the Tower. While in prison he had made a vow that, if it should please God to release him, he would "return unto Him by some holy and pious employment, that summe and more, by which of His gracious providence was unexpectedly conveyed in unto me during my eighteen years captivity."

Wren's " holy and pious employment " took the form of building a new chapel for Pembroke " in a grateful remembrance of his first education which was in that Place received." The architect was the benefactor's nephew, and Pembroke Chapel has thus become famous in the history of architecture as the first work of Sir Christopher Wren. To link the new chapel with the college a cloister, with chambers above it, was built in 1666. This cloister was consecrated with a view to the burial in it of students who died in college, and it now contains a series of stone tablets on which are recorded the names of 300 Pembroke men who fell in the War of 1914–18.

Further additions to the college building were also made in the seventeenth century. These consisted of two ranges of chambers running east of the hall and forming a court which came to be known as Ivy Court. Recently the ivy has been ruthlessly torn from the walls—an act which horrified the sentimentalists, but was welcomed by lovers of seventeenth-century brickwork.

On the completion of Wren's chapel, the old chapel became a library, and although a new library was built in 1875, the bookcases and the magnificent plaster-work ceiling (1690) of the " Old Library " still remain.

Another fine ceiling was recently added to the college fabric, the neo-Gothic roof of the hall being removed and the hall itself enlarged by the inclusion of the old Combination Room. In 1932 the elaborate, but unlovely, Master's Lodge of 1874 was converted into undergraduates' rooms and a new lodge built in a corner of the fellows' garden.

It was another Pembroke which Johnson called " a nest of singing-birds," but poets have flourished at the Cambridge Pembroke. Chief among them are Spenser and Gray. Spenser entered the college in 1569, and an ancient mulberry-

tree in the college garden is proudly known as " Spenser's
Mulberry-Tree." The history of this ancient tree, which was
almost certainly planted in the sixteenth, or in the seventeenth century, is obscure, but the garden with its bowling-
green and its avenue of noble plane-trees in which the owls
still hoot, needs no " associations " to commend it. Gray,
having once migrated to Pembroke, lived there for the greater
part of his life :

" The Spirit of Lazyness (the Spirit of the Place) begins
to possess even me, that have so long declaimed against it :
yet has it not so prevail'd, but that I feel that discontent
with myself, that *Ennuy*, that ever accompanies it in its
Beginnings. Time will settle my Conscience, time will re-
concile me to this languid Companion : we shall smoke, we
shall tipple, we shall doze together, we shall ·have our little
Jokes, like other People, and our long Stories ; Brandy will
finish what Port begun . . ."

Gray's letters, which are not to be taken too seriously,
throw many side-lights on eighteenth-century college life—
the quarrels of the fellows and the paucity of undergraduates.
His rooms, afterwards occupied by William Pitt and E. G.
Browne, were in the south-west corner of Ivy Court, and
everybody in Pembroke, he said, was as civil to him as they
could be to Mary de Valence in person.

One of Gray's intimate friends was William Mason, who
was elected a Fellow in 1749 ; Mason may be reckoned
among the many minor poets of Pembroke, and Gray took
infinite pains in criticising the draft of his *Caractacus*.
Amongst other Pembroke poets are Gabriel Harvey, the
friend of Spenser ; Richard Crashaw, " Poet and Saint,"
who migrated to Peterhouse ; and Christopher Smart, of
whom a recently-acquired portrait may be seen in the Hall.
Kit Smart's college patriotism is shown in a *Jubilee Ode*

which he wrote in 1743, it being then believed that the college had been founded in 1343:

> Religious joy, and sober pleasure,
> Virtuous ease, and learned leisure,
> Society and books, that give
> Th' important lesson how to live:
> These are gifts, are gifts divine,
> For, fair Pembroke, these were thine.

But Pembroke, the *Collegium Episcopale*, was the home of bishops and martyrs even before it produced its poets. Richard Fox, Bishop of Winchester and Founder of Corpus Christi College, Oxford, was Master from 1507-1519; Ridley held the same office from 1540 to 1553. "In thy orchard," he wrote in his famous *Farewell* to Pembroke, "(the wals, buts and trees, if they could speake, would beare me witnes) I learned without booke almost all Paules epistles." Thomas Nevile went from Pembroke to be Master, first of Magdalene and afterwards of Trinity; Whitgift, too, was a Pembroke man and Master for a short time before he went to Trinity. Lancelot Andrewes was Master for a longer period, 1589–1605.

In the eighteenth century the greatest curiosity in the college was:

"Dr Long's machine, or tin-plate sphere, exhibiting all the circles and the appearance of the heavens, erected for the meridian of Cambridge. It is eighteen feet in diameter, so that thirty persons might sit in it, and on the turning of a winch may see the actual appearance, the relative situation, and successive motions of the heavenly bodies."

This was the work of Roger Long, Master from 1733 to 1770, and famous for his astronomical and musical pursuits, "the high and mighty Prince Roger" as Gray calls him, "surnamed the Long, Lord of the great Zodiack, the Glass Uranium, and the Chariot that goes without Horses."

But a more famous name in the annals of eighteenth-century Pembroke is that of the younger Pitt, who was admitted in 1773. Lord Chatham's letter introducing his son to the college has fortunately been preserved. "Apprehensions of gout" prevented the father from escorting his son to Cambridge, and he accordingly sketched the boy's qualities:

"He is of a tender Age and of a health not yet firm enough to be indulged, to the full, in the strong desire he has, to acquire knowledge. An ingenuous mind and docility of temper will, I know, render him conformable to your Discipline in all points. Too young for the irregularities of a man, I trust, he will not, on the other hand, prove troublesome by the Puerile sallies of a Boy. Such as he is, I am happy to place him at Pembroke."

Pitt's name is commemorated in Pembroke in a block of buildings built in 1908 to the north-east of Ivy Court and in the University by the famous neo-Gothic building on the other side of Trumpington Street, known as the Pitt Press. This was built in 1831 out of the surplus of the fund raised for erecting a statue of Pitt in London. It is the most prominent, but not the most useful, part of the University Press, and its ecclesiastical appearance gave rise to its other name, "the Freshmen's Church," the church, that is, at which freshmen were advised to attend divine service on their first Sunday.

Sir George Gabriel Stokes, one of the greatest of Pembroke mathematicians, came up in the year of Victoria's accession and became Master in the year after her death. Throughout his long life he preserved some of the habits of the older Cambridge—the "Grantchester Grind" and the enjoyment of two meals in the day. Like Newton, he represented the University in Parliament, but made no speeches; to the House of Commons of 1886 he appeared as the most remarkable of all Members—a silent Irishman.

CORPUS CHRISTI COLLEGE: A CORNER OF THE OLD COURT

CORPUS CHRISTI COLLEGE

TO cross Pembroke Street is to enter within the limits of mediæval Cambridge, for along the line of this street ran the King's Ditch, and at its junction with Trumpington Street there stood the Trumpington Gate, built in 1267 by King Henry III. The first church within the gates is that of St Botolph, the patron saint of travellers, and next to it is the College of Corpus Christi and the Blessed Virgin Mary. Corpus is unique in having grown out of the combination in 1352 of two gilds, those of Corpus Christi and the Blessed Virgin. Originally the foundation consisted of a Master and two Fellows, who were responsible for the education of secular priests who should celebrate masses for the souls of departed members of the gilds. For two hundred years St Benet's Church, whose noble Saxon tower still stands, served as a college chapel and gave the name of " Benet " to the college. Like Pembroke, the college originally consisted of one small court ; but Corpus, more fortunate than its neighbour, has preserved its Old Court almost intact. On three sides the fourteenth-century sets of chambers remain. On the other side the old hall has become the kitchen, and the old master's lodging has been converted into sets of rooms for undergraduates. Thus the Old Court of Corpus remains the oldest complete court in Cambridge. Until a few years ago it was not only ancient, but picturesque, since its walls were almost completely covered with ivy. But now the ivy

4

has wisely been removed, and those who seek in Cambridge for " the last enchantments of the Middle Age " may well begin (with their backs to the present Hall) in the Old Court of Corpus.

Additions were made to the college buildings in the sixteenth century, consisting of a chapel, a master's gallery and a tennis-court; but these have disappeared, and the New Court which fronts forbiddingly upon Trumpington Street was the work of William Wilkins in 1823–26. With a keen eye for symmetry, Wilkins perceived that the sixteenth-century chapel would not be exactly in line with the middle of his proposed range of buildings. The old chapel, therefore, was demolished, and the new chapel was built with its west door in strict alignment with the entrance gateway. Centrality was achieved.

The new court also contains, on the upper floor of its south side, a library of international renown. This is the collection of Matthew Parker, Master of the college from 1544 to 1553, and afterwards Archbishop of Canterbury. It was Parker's wife whom Elizabeth thanked for her hospitality in a famous sentence: " Madam I may not call you; Mistress I am ashamed to call you; so I know not what to call you; but yet I do thank you."

Parker was a " mighty collector " of books and manuscripts and took pains, in particular, to preserve the treasures of learning which were in danger of being dispersed and lost after the dissolution of the monasteries. He bequeathed his collection to his college, making strict provision that if either six folios, eight quartos, or twelve smaller books should at any time be missing for more than six months, the collection should be forfeited to Gonville and Caius College. Similar neglect by Caius was to be punished by forfeiture to Trinity Hall. In Parker's collection the

manuscripts are more famous than the printed books.
Among them are Jerome's Latin version of the *Four Gospels*,
written early in the seventh century and sent by Pope
Gregory to Augustine at Canterbury; several copies of the
Anglo-Saxon Chronicle; an Anglo-Saxon version of the *Four
Gospels*; a folio MS of the *Iliad* and *Odyssey*, rescued from
St Augustine's monastery at Canterbury; and Matthew
Paris's own copy of his *History*. To Parker the college also
owes much of its magnificent plate, but still more famous
is the Wassail Horn, " a great horn, with feet silver gilt and
the head of an emperor at the end, silver gilt; having also
a silver cover, at the top of which are four acorns, silver
gilt." This horn was given to the Gild of Corpus Christi
about 1347 by John Goldcorne, alderman of the Gild, and
was used at feasts of the Gild before the foundation of the
college. It is still used at college feasts, and, as many
guests of the college have realised, "needs peculiar hand-
ling in a back-handed fashion, with the two silver feet resting
upon the arm above the elbows, and a good lift of the right
hand."

Many famous names, besides that of Parker, are found
in the annals of Corpus in the sixteenth century, such as
those of Sir Nicholas Bacon, Keeper of the Great Seal;
Thomas Cavendish, the circumnavigator; Robert Browne,
the founder of Congregationalism; John Robinson, pastor
of the Pilgrim Fathers; Christopher Marlowe and John
Fletcher, the dramatists. Not much is known of Kit
Marlowe's career beyond the fact that he was in almost
continual residence between 1581 and 1587, and recently his
name has been commemorated on a stone panel in the Old
Court.

In later centuries Corpus was true to its archiepiscopal
tradition. Thomas Tenison, who entered the college in 1653

and became a Fellow six years later, was Rector for some years of St Martin's-in-the-Fields, where he preached the funeral sermon on Nell Gwynne. A great benefactor to London charities, he succeeded Tillotson as Archbishop of Canterbury in 1694. Thomas Herring, who came to Corpus from Jesus in 1716, was successively Archbishop of York and of Canterbury.

" To those who will look over the list of members of this Society," wrote William Cole, the antiquary, " it will be obvious to see that they have occupied places in Church and State, equal to those of more ample foundations."

In addition to famous men, Corpus may lay claim to the most famous ghost in Cambridge. Its habitat is that corner of the Old Court in which the old Lodge has been converted into undergraduates' rooms ; its personality is less certain, being associated, according to one story, with the unfortunate Dr Butts who was Master in the plague year of 1630, " a destitute and forsaken man," and was found hanging by his garters on Easter Day 1632 when he should have been preaching the University Sermon. The other story connects the ghost with an equally unfortunate young man who was paying court to the daughter of John Spencer (Master from 1667 to 1693), and, being interrupted in his wooing, took hasty refuge in an adjacent cupboard where he died miserably.

As recently as 1904 an undergraduate, living opposite to the haunted rooms, is said to have seen the head and shoulders of the ghost, whose features were " those of a stranger with long hair." Shortly afterwards a party of six tried their hands at exorcism. Prayers were recited and the spirit was ordered to appear. Two of the six saw the ghost, which came " in the form of a mist of about a yard wide, which slowly developed into the form of a man who

seemed to be shrouded in white, and had a gash in his neck." [1]
The two men endeavoured, with the aid of a crucifix, to drive
the spirit away, but broke down in a state of collapse.   Since
that time there has been no further psychical disturbance in
Old Court.

[1] *Occult Review*, March, 1905.

ST CATHARINE'S COLLEGE—QUEENS' COLLEGE

QUEENS' COLLEGE: THE PRESIDENT'S LODGE

ST CATHARINE'S COLLEGE—QUEENS' COLLEGE

IMMEDIATELY opposite Corpus is St Catharine's, with its three-sided court uniquely open to the street. Until a few years ago a famous row of elms stood in front of it, and the hoot of the screech-owl was a familiar noise at night.

Founded in 1473 by Robert Wodelarke, Provost of King's, " to the honour of God, the most blessed Virgin Mary, and saint Katerine the virgin . . . for one master and a certain number of fellows, to last for ever to the praise of God and the establishment of the faith," the college has preserved practically nothing of its original fabric. The component parts of the court as it stands to-day belong to various periods of the seventeenth and eighteenth centuries and have been welded into a remarkable unity. The fine Renaissance gateway on the far side is actually the entrance gateway, since the college originally faced towards what is now Queens' Lane but was once Milne Street, the main highway of the town. Between the college and Trumpington Street there stood, until 1757, a row of houses, and, though it had been proposed to complete the court a century before, the fourth side of the court was never built. Now, however, a new block has been built in continuation of the north wing and will some day have its fellow on the south.

James Shirley, the dramatist, graduated at St Catharine's

5

in 1618, and his contemporary, Thomas Bancroft, the epi-
grammatist, alludes to the " precious yeeres " spent by them
both under St Catharine's wheel. John Ray, " father of
natural history in this country," entered the college in 1644,
but afterwards migrated to Trinity. From St Catharine's,
too, came John Addenbrooke, who, in 1719, bequeathed
money " to erect and maintain a small physical hospital "—
an institution which has grown to be of the first importance
both to the town and the university.

On the other side of Queens' Lane stands the college
which gives the lane its name. Only Cambridge men—and
not all of them—can be trusted to spell the name of the college
correctly, since two queens of England are commemorated
in it. The original founder was, in fact, Andrew Doket,
who obtained a royal charter in 1446 for the establishment
of " the college of St Bernard in Cambridge." Two years
later a second charter was obtained, and Queen Margaret,
" beholding her husband's bounty in building King's College
was restless in herself with holy emulation until she had
produced something of the like nature, a strife wherein wives
without breach of duty may contend with their husbands
which should exceed in pious performances." [1] The Queen
was accordingly granted the " foundation and denomination "
of the college. On the accession of Edward IV, Elizabeth
Woodville similarly took the college under her protection,
and so the college has been described as the first outward
symbol of the reconciliation of Lancaster and York.

Queens' is fortunate in that its original court, built in
deep red brick with a turret at each corner, has been preserved almost in its entirety. Queens' Lane is too narrow
to enable the gateway to be properly seen, but the whole

[1] Thomas Fuller.

QUEENS' COLLEGE: THE WOODEN BRIDGE

court is a good example of the fifteenth-century collegiate plan, based upon that of the English gentleman's country mansion: chambers, kitchen, butteries, hall, master's lodging, library, and chapel. Over the entrance of the old chapel (now used as a lecture-room and library) is a famous sun-dial. The present dial, which replaced an older one of 1642, was erected in 1733. Legend connects it with Sir Isaac Newton, but Newton died in 1728. Cole, the Cambridge antiquary of the eighteenth century, rightly describes it as " a very elegant Sun Dial with all ye signs," and as " no small ornamᵗ to ye Court to enliven it."

The second, or Cloister Court, is perhaps one of the most surprising, and certainly one of the most beautiful, in Cambridge. One side of it, the river side, is almost as old as the first court, having been built in the same dark brick about 1460. Cloisters, also in brick, run round three sides, but the great glory of the court is the Gallery of the President's Lodge. Built in two storeys, eighty feet long and twelve feet wide, it is balanced upon beams laid across the walls of the cloister. Until 1911 the walls of the Gallery were plastered right over, but now the sixteenth-century timber work is revealed in its mellowed beauty, and the whole building is an almost perfect example of Tudor domestic architecture.

One of the early Presidents of Queens' was John Fisher, the first Lady Margaret's Professor of Divinity and Bishop of Rochester. He was made Chancellor of the University in 1504, and in the following year came to Queens' as its President. It was at the invitation of Fisher that Erasmus entered the college about 1510, and tradition connects his residence with the turret in the south-west corner of the Principal Court. No doubt he had more than the turret-room at his disposal, but the tower still retains its name of " Erasmus' Tower." Here Erasmus worked upon the New

Testament and upon his edition of St Jerome, and when tired of study " for lacke of better exercise he would take his horse and ryde about the Market Hill." Appointed Reader in Greek to the University, Erasmus was disappointed in the paucity of his hearers. In 1511 he succeeded Fisher in the Lady Margaret's Chair of Divinity, and his letters written from Cambridge are like those of Thomas Gray in that the complaints need not be taken too seriously. The students, according to Erasmus, were poverty-stricken ; the townsmen boorish ; the beer unsatisfactory. College patriots have been careful to point out that *cervisia huius loci* must refer to the beer, not of Queens' in particular, but of Cambridge in general. However, Erasmus had at least a good word for the Cambridge school of theology :

" In the University of Cambridge, instead of sophistical arguments, their theologians debate in a sober, sensible manner and depart wiser and better men."

It may well have been Erasmus who was responsible for the introduction of printing into Cambridge. Certainly John Siberch, who in 1521 printed the first Cambridge book (an *Oration* by Henry Bullock, Fellow of Queens', on the occasion of Wolsey's visit), was one of Erasmus' friends, and all the evidence supports the conjecture that he came to Cambridge at Erasmus' invitation.

A little later in the sixteenth century the fame of Sir Thomas Smith (Fellow of Queens' in 1530, and afterwards Secretary of State in the reigns of Edward VI and Elizabeth), was such that " Queens' College carried away the glory for eloquence from all the Colleges besides, and was rendered so famous by this her scholar, that it had like to have changed her name from Queens' to Smith's College."

In the next century one of the most genial worthies of Queens' was Thomas Fuller, the historian of the University

and the author of *The Holy State, The Worthies of England,*
and many other works. In the characters drawn in *The
Holy State* Fuller was not slow to use his powers of university
observation. Of " The good Master of a Colledge " he
writes :

" *His learning if beneath eminency is farre above contempt.*
Sometimes ordinary scholars make extraordinary good
Masters. Every one who can play well on Apollo's harp
cannot skilfully drive his chariot, there being a peculiar
mystery of Government. Yea as a little alloy makes gold
to work the better, so (perchance) some dulnesse in a
man makes him fitter to manage secular affairs. . . ."

Queens', says George Dyer, " has been rather famous
for mathematicians and divines than poets," and its bridge
which leads from the Cloister Court to the Grove on the
other side of the river is commonly known as the " Mathematical Bridge." Like the sun-dial, it is commonly, but
erroneously, attributed to Sir Isaac Newton. It is, however,
true that the construction of the first wooden bridge, built
about 1700, may have owed something to Newton. It was
replaced by the present bridge in 1749.

From the Grove the traveller should be careful to turn
his eyes down, not up, the river. In the latter direction he
will see only the unlovely iron bridge, the dismantled mill
beyond, and the incongruous corner of Queens' built by James
Essex, the Cambridge architect, in 1760. Essex was " well
versed in what was then specially distinguished as 'regular
architecture,' " and has left his mark upon many college
courts.

But in the other direction one may begin, from the Grove
of Queens', to see something of the greatest of the charms
of Cambridge—the relation of the colleges to the river.
Immediately in front there is the mellowed brick-work of

the Queens' river-front ; just beyond is the wall of the President's garden ; and beyond there are the bridges of King's and Clare and the pinnacles of the chapel of King's. It is a view which was one hundred years ago described as " one of the best anywhere ; for it has grand objects, which amply compensate for the want of other beauties ; a small home view, with the accompaniment of magnificent edifices, and agreeable scenery."

KING'S AND CLARE COLLEGES: FROM THE BACKS

KING'S COLLEGE

KING'S COLLEGE CHAPEL: WEST END

KING'S COLLEGE

WALKING to the end of Queens' Lane, the traveller may enter King's by a side-door, and, finding his way through a labyrinth of modern buildings, he will come suddenly upon one of the most splendid views in Cambridge—the southern façade of Clare seen across the great lawn of King's. For the present, however, let him turn to the right and see a yet more famous façade—the south side of the chapel of King's. Even the visitor who rushes through Cambridge in half an hour must take away some impression of

> " That branching roof
> Self-poised, and scooped into ten thousand cells,
> Where light and shade repose, where music dwells
> Lingering—and wandering on as loth to die ;
> Like thoughts whose very sweetness yieldeth proof
> That they were born for immortality."

The rose and portcullis, first seen over the south doorway, commemorate the work of Henry VII, but the royal founder was Henry VI, who, in his double foundation of Eton and King's, followed the plan of William of Wykeham, who had established Winchester and New College, Oxford, some seventy years before. In 1441 the building of King's was begun, and the only relic of the original college is to be seen in what is now the back gate of the University Library. Here the " Old Court " (the original nucleus of Henry VI's college) stood until 1835, when the site was purchased by

6   41

or persons he may think fit to Gothicise Gibbs's Building, according to the plan originally proposed by Mr Wilkins." Fortunately this plan was not carried out, and the work of James Gibbs remains unviolated by the crude Gothicism of 1830. To-day the pendulum has swung the other way: a new Lodge has been provided for the Provost and that built by Wilkins is marked for demolition.

From the beginning King's has held a peculiar position in the university. Henry VI made it independent not only of the Bishop of Ely, but also of the Chancellor and Masters of the University, and until the middle of the nineteenth century a " King's Scholar " of Eton proceeded to a scholarship at King's and afterwards passed, without examination, to a Bachelor's degree and a Fellowship, which he held for life. But since 1861 the college has been open to non-Etonians, and now insists only that its students shall read for honours, and not for a pass degree.

If King's has had rather less than its share of major poets, it has at least produced a remarkable variety of verse. Giles Fletcher, Elizabeth's ambassador to Russia, wrote a Latin poem, *De Litteris antiquæ Britanniæ*, which includes an account of Cambridge; his son, Phineas, was the author of *The Purple Island* (1633), an allegorical poem put into the mouth of a shepherd who tells his tale

> " where by the orchard walls
> The learned Chame with stealing water crawls,
> And lowly down before that royal temple falls."

As an undergraduate, Phineas sometimes grew weary of the Cambridge country; in 1601 he wrote to his cousin:

> " Here must I stay, in sullen study pent,
>   Among our Cambridge fens my time misspending;
> But then revisit our long long'd-for Kent
>   Till then live happy, the time ever mending."

KING'S COLLEGE

WALKING to the end of Queens' Lane, the traveller may enter King's by a side-door, and, finding his way through a labyrinth of modern buildings, he will come suddenly upon one of the most splendid views in Cambridge—the southern façade of Clare seen across the great lawn of King's. For the present, however, let him turn to the right and see a yet more famous façade—the south side of the chapel of King's. Even the visitor who rushes through Cambridge in half an hour must take away some impression of

> " That branching roof
> Self-poised, and scooped into ten thousand cells,
> Where light and shade repose, where music dwells
> Lingering—and wandering on as loth to die ;
> Like thoughts whose very sweetness yieldeth proof
> That they were born for immortality."

The rose and portcullis, first seen over the south doorway, commemorate the work of Henry VII, but the royal founder was Henry VI, who, in his double foundation of Eton and King's, followed the plan of William of Wykeham, who had established Winchester and New College, Oxford, some seventy years before. In 1441 the building of King's was begun, and the only relic of the original college is to be seen in what is now the back gate of the University Library. Here the " Old Court " (the original nucleus of Henry VI's college) stood until 1835, when the site was purchased by the University. This original court was, in fact, never finished, since the Provost and Fellows of Henry's foundation complained that it would not provide sufficient accommodation. The King accordingly secured a much larger site between the river and the High Street, enclosing several of the lanes which connected the two, and sweeping away the church of St John Zachary, an inn called the Boar's Head, and several hostels and tenements.

The first stone of the chapel was laid by the King in 1446, and two years later he drew up a document called the *Will of King Henry VI*, in which the dimensions and the manner of building were very clearly specified :

" I haue deuised and appointed that the same chirch shal conteyne in lengthe 288 fete of assyse, withoute any yles and alle of the widenesse of 40 fete . . . also a reredos beryng the Rodeloft departyng the quere and the body of the chirch, conteynyng in lengthe 40 fete and in brede 14 fete ; the walls of the same chirche to be in height 90 fete, embatelled, vauted, and chare rofed sufficiently boteraced and euery boterace fined with finialx. . . . And I wol that the edificacion of my same College procede in large fourme clene and substancial, settyng a parte superfluite of too gret curious werkes of entaille and besy moldyng. . . ."

The chapel was the only part of Henry's scheme of buildings which was actually carried out, and it was about seventy years before it was finished. One or two of the side chapels were in use in 1470, but it was not until the end of the reign of Henry VII that the work was resumed in earnest. By 1515 the stone fabric was completed, and shortly afterwards fresh glory was added to the chapel by the stained glass of the windows. The contract stipulated that they should represent " the story of the olde lawe and of the newe lawe, after the fourme, maner, goodnes, curyousytie, and clenlynes in euery poynt of the glasse wyndowes of the kynges newe Chapell at Westmynster " ; and this plan was carried out by depicting events from the New Testament in the lower tier, with scenes from the Old Testament and the Apocrypha above. Finally, the stalls, screen, and rood-loft were provided by Henry VIII, the screen being one of the earliest examples of Renaissance wood-work in England.

To-day King's College Chapel has become something more than a college building. Every Cambridge man has a fraction of reverent pride in its outstanding beauty. Within its walls the devotee and the musician, the æsthete and the sentimentalist can meet on common ground.

In the early part of the eighteenth century plans were prepared for a new court to be built with the chapel as its north side. Only one block, however, was built, and fortunately this was entrusted to James Gibbs, who succeeded in erecting a building " with the air and grandeur of a Roman palace " which could stand without offence alongside the final triumph of the English Perpendicular style. Gibbs built in the spirit, though not in the style, of Henry VI's *Will* ; he set apart superfluity of too great curious works of entail and busy moulding and confined his ornament to the pediment of the noble archway in the middle of his building.

The same cannot be said of the other sides of the court. Between 1824 and 1828 the same Wilkins who built the New Court of Corpus built the hall, library, and Provost's Lodge of King's as well as the stone screen which is seen from the street. It was the heyday of the Gothic revival, and it was felt, no doubt, that the college must have a front elevation worthy of the chapel. The Provost was even authorised to " enter into another Contract with any person or persons he may think fit to Gothicise Gibbs's Building, according to the plan originally proposed by Mr Wilkins." Fortunately this plan was not carried out, and the work of James Gibbs remains unviolated by the crude Gothicism of 1830. To-day the pendulum has swung the other way : a new Lodge has been provided for the Provost and that built by Wilkins is marked for demolition.

From the beginning King's has held a peculiar position in the university. Henry VI made it independent not only of the Bishop of Ely, but also of the Chancellor and Masters of the University, and until the middle of the nineteenth century a " King's Scholar " of Eton proceeded to a scholarship at King's and afterwards passed, without examination, to a Bachelor's degree and a Fellowship, which he held for life. But since 1861 the college has been open to non-Etonians, and now insists only that its students shall read for honours, and not for a pass degree.

If King's has had rather less than its share of major poets, it has at least produced a remarkable variety of verse. Giles Fletcher, Elizabeth's ambassador to Russia, wrote a Latin poem, *De Litteris antiquæ Britanniæ*, which includes an account of Cambridge ; his son, Phineas, was the author of *The Purple Island* (1633), an allegorical poem put into the mouth of a shepherd who tells his tale

> " where by the orchard walls
> The learned Chame with stealing water crawls,
> And lowly down before that royal temple falls."

As an undergraduate, Phineas sometimes grew weary of the Cambridge country ; in 1601 he wrote to his cousin :

> " Here must I stay, in sullen study pent,
>   Among our Cambridge fens my time misspending ;
> But then revisit our long long'd-for Kent
>   Till then live happy, the time ever mending."

KING'S COLLEGE CHAPEL: SOUTH DOOR

Edmund Waller, who entered the college in 1621, had a varied political career, in the course of which he wrote congratulatory verses to Charles II as well as a panegyric on Cromwell. " He was," said Johnson, " rather smooth than strong. . . . His thoughts are such as a liberal conversation and large acquaintance with life would easily supply."

The most famous of Eton poets went to another college, but Gray knew something of King's from his friend Horace Walpole, who was admitted as a fellow-commoner in 1734-5. Gray, Ashton, Walpole, and West formed a " quadruple alliance " of literary friendship.

" Dear West " (wrote Walpole on 9th November 1735), " You expect a long letter from me and have said in verse all that I intended to have said in far inferior prose. I intended filling three or four sides with exclamations against an university life, but you have showed me how strongly they may be expressed in three or four lines. I can't build without straw ; nor have I the ingenuity of the spider to spin fine lines out of dirt : a master of a college would make but a miserable figure as a hero of a poem. . . ."

Like Gray, Walpole set a low value upon mathematical studies :

" But why mayn't we hold a classical correspondence ? I can never forget the many agreeable hours we have passed in reading Horace and Virgil ; and I think they are topics will never grow stale. Let us extend the Roman empire, and cultivate two barbarous towns o'er-run with rusticity and mathematics. . . . We have not the least poetry stirring here. . . ."

Later in the eighteenth century a Kingsman was stirred to poetry of an unconventional kind. This was Christopher Anstey, who became a Fellow in 1745. Three years later he was summoned to declaim in Latin in the Schools before proceeding to the degree of Master of Arts. Resenting this as an attack on a Kingsman's privilege, he began his declamation with words of ridicule, and was suspended from his degree ; his second speech (which is said to have opened with " Doctores sine doctrina, Magistri Artium sine Artibus ") was similarly unsatisfactory, and Anstey afterwards wrote of

> " Granta, sweet Granta, where studious of ease
> Seven years did I sleep, and then lost my degrees."

In 1766 Anstey, who had succeeded to an estate at Trumpington, leapt into popular fame with the *New Bath Guide*, a gay collection of epistolary verses " written by a family during their residence at Bath," and showing as little respect for academic dignity as the Latin declamations :

> " Dean Spavin, Dean Mangey, and Doctor De'squirt
> Were all sent from *Cambridge* to rub off their dirt."

It is a far cry from Christopher Anstey to Rupert Brooke. Yet *The Old Vicarage, Grantchester* was first written for, and published in, an undergraduate magazine, and Anstey might have liked the description of the vicarage garden :

> " And in that garden, black and white,
> Creep whispers through the grass all night ;
> And spectral dance, before the dawn,
> A hundred Vicars down the lawn ;
> Curates, long dust, will come and go
> On lissom, clerical, printless toe ;
> And oft between the boughs is seen
> The sly shade of a Rural Dean. . . ."

Of eighteenth-century Kingsmen the most famous was a clergyman very different from Anstey. This was Charles Simeon, the great evangelical divine who was admitted a scholar in 1779. Determined to spread a new gospel of religious discipline and evangelical devotion, he first practised it himself : if he failed to rise for prayer and study at four o'clock in the morning, he paid a fine of half-a-crown to his bedmaker ; if that stimulus failed, he went down to the river and threw a guinea into it. In 1783 he became Vicar of Holy Trinity. The parishioners were violently opposed to the appointment, and when Simeon proposed to establish an " evening lecture," the churchwardens locked up the church. Simeon took a smith with him to open the doors. For many years Holy Trinity Church was the scene of constant riots, in spite of the efforts of the Proctors and of " persons furnished with white wands " to preserve order in and around the church. But in the end Simeon triumphed. " If you knew," wrote Macaulay, " what his authority and influence were, and how they extended from Cambridge to the most remote corners of England, you would allow that his real sway over the Church was far greater than that of any primate."

Nineteenth-century King's was rich in " characters," and what more can a college desire ? Many of them—Oscar Browning, Walter Headlam, J. E. Nixon—have been recently portrayed, with deft economy of description, by Dr M. R. James,[1] and more elaborate pictures may be found in the novels of Mr E. F. Benson, Mr E. M. Forster, and others.

But no page of fiction is so strange as the description of the election of a Provost in 1742 :

" The Fellows went into Chapel on Monday before noon in the morning as the Statute directs. After prayers and sacrament, they began to vote—22 for George ; 16 for Thackeray ; 10 for Chapman."

" Thus they continued, scrutinizing, and walking about, eating, and sleeping ; some of them smoaking. Still the same numbers for each candidate ; till yesterday about

[1] *Eton and King's* (1926).

noon (for they held that in the 48 hours allowed for the Election no adjournment could be made) ; when the Tories, Chapman's friends, refusing absolutely to concur with either of the two other parties, Thackeray's votes went over to George by agreement, and he was declared.

" A friend of mine, a curious man, tells me, he took a survey of his brothers at the hour of two in the morning ; and that never was a more curious, or a more diverting spectacle.

" Some wrapped in blankets, erect in their stalls like mummies : others, asleep on cushions, like so many Gothic tombs.   Here a red cap over a wig ; there a face lost in the cape of a rug.   One blowing a chafing dish with a surplice sleeve ; another warming a little negus, or sipping Coke upon Littleton, *i.e.* tent and brandy.   Thus did they combat the cold of that frosty night ; which has not killed any one of them, to my infinite surprize."

CLARE COLLEGE, FROM THE AVENUE

CLARE COLLEGE

CLARE COLLEGE

TO pass from King's College Chapel into the old court (till recently the only court) of Clare is to pass from the culmination of English Perpendicular Gothic to what the late Professor Willis described as "one of the most beautiful buildings, from its situation and general outline, that he could point out in the University. It had a homogeneous appearance, more like a palace than a College."

Founded by the University as University Hall in 1326, and refounded by Lady Elizabeth de Clare as Clare Hall in 1338, the college was rebuilt in the seventeenth century. The work was begun in 1638, and, after interruptions due to the Civil War, was eventually completed in 1715. Students of architecture may thus discern differences of style in various portions of the work, but the ordinary observer will be primarily impressed by the graceful unity of the whole court.

According to the canons of taste which prevailed in the early nineteenth century, the building was not wholly satisfactory. "A brightness, a neatness, a uniformity, with something of elegance" were conceded to it, but it was felt that "the edifice had in general too much of little ornament for the chaste classical style." To-day, the Jacobean quality of the nameless architect of Clare is better appreciated.

The river-front is somewhat obscured by an overgrowth

of trees ; but the bridge (built in 1640 by Thomas Grumbold, a master-mason) is a lovely structure, and the lovelier for the slight subsidence of the central arch. One of the stone balls which are ranged along the parapets has been a source of delight to many generations of tourists, in that it shows a slice neatly cut out of it as out of a pudding.[1]

The bridge leads through a gate of elegant iron-work, made about 1714, to an avenue of limes, with the Fellows' Garden on the north. Here, until 1925, the college domain ended. In that year, just before the celebration of the six hundredth anniversary of the foundation of the college, the first block of the Memorial Building, designed by Sir Giles Gilbert Scott, was opened. Built in grey brick, with a lofty entrance gateway, the Memorial Building is the first example of an old college spreading to the other side of the Backs.

The history of Clare, especially its ecclesiastical history, goes back, of course, a long way behind the present buildings. Hugh Latimer was elected a Fellow in 1510, and it was from Clare that he went across the road to St Edward's Church to preach his famous " Sermons on the Card " in 1529 :

" And whereas you are wont to celebrate Christmas in playing at cards, I intend, by God's grace, to deal unto you Christ's cards, wherein you shall perceive Christ's rule.. . . . Then further we must say to ourselves, ' What requireth Christ of a christian man ? ' Now turn up your trump, your heart (hearts is trump, as I said before), and cast your trump, your heart, on this card ; and upon this card you shall learn what Christ requireth of a christian man—not to be angry, ne moved to ire against his neighbour, in mind, countenance, nor other ways, by word or deed."

[1] One story told in explanation is that a King's man threw one of the centre balls into the river ; and that this was replaced by a ball taken from the south-west corner of the bridge where it had been cut to fit into the angle of the wall.

" This blunt preaching," says Fuller, " was in those dark days admirably effectual."

Nicholas Ferrar, who was admitted to the college at the age of thirteen in 1606, was a youth of such attractive personality that at the end of his first year the Fellows " would needs have him Fellow-commoner that he might be their companion." Ferrar embarked at first upon a public career and was elected to Parliament in 1624. When the plague broke out in 1625, however, he retired to Little Gidding, in Huntingdonshire, and there remained as a kind of abbot presiding over a Protestant monastery, composed of the families of his brother and his brother-in-law. Work upon the Scriptures occupied much of the time of this " Arminian nunnery," and Charles I insisted on having copies of the Little Gidding Concordances. Ferrar died in 1637.

Another seventeenth-century Fellow of Clare who attracted royal attention was George Ruggle, author of a Latin play *Ignoramus*, a satirical attack upon the legal profession. James I was so much pleased by it when he saw it acted in Clare in 1614 that he came to Cambridge again to see a second performance. The lawyers were furious at the King's appreciation.

" Oxford comicke Actours had ; Cambridge a lawyer foole
Who Ignoramus christen'd was by men of her own schoole
Oxford acts in toto were well pleasing unto some ;
But Ignoramus pleased best the Kinge when it was done."

A later Stuart monarch was less pleased with a Fellow of Clare, for when Nathaniel Vincent preached before Charles II at Newmarket in a long periwig and holland sleeves (" according to the then fashion for Gentlemen ") on 4th October 1674, his Majesty was greatly shocked, and commanded the Duke of Monmouth, then Chancellor of the University, to issue a suitable reprimand. The Chancellor accordingly acquainted the University with his Majesty's displeasure at persons in holy orders " wearing their hair and perukes of an unusual and unbecoming length," and further ordering preachers before the University to deliver their sermons, both Latin and English, " by memory or without book, as being a way of preaching which his Majesty judgeth most agreeable to the use of all foreign churches, to the custom of the University heretofore, and the nature and intendment of that holy exercise."

More famous figures in seventeenth-century Clare were those of Peter Gunning and John Tillotson. Gunning was a stout Royalist, and preached the royal cause with great effect at Little St Mary's. Imprisoned and deprived of his fellowship during the Civil War, he was made Master of Clare at the Restoration. Both Evelyn and Pepys were enthusiastic in their praise of the sermons of this " incomparable hammer of the schismatics." Tillotson, who became a Fellow of Clare in 1651, was similarly known as " the best polemical divine in England," and was credited with " having brought preaching to perfection." He became Archbishop of Canterbury in 1694.

A less fortunate preacher, who was also a member of Clare, was Dr William Dodd, who was hanged at Tyburn for forging a bond on his patron, Lord Chesterfield, in spite of the efforts made by Johnson on his behalf. Amongst other pieces, Johnson wrote for Dodd his *Last Solemn Declaration* :

" Vanity and pleasure required expence disproportionate to my income. Expence brought distress upon me, and distress impelled me to fraud.

" For this fraud I am to die ; and I die declaring that however I have taught others to the best of my knowledge the true way to eternal happiness. My life has been hypocritical, but my ministry has been sincere."

Never has the road to ruin been more concisely, or more fairly, summarised.

Clare is not rich in poets, but can claim a poet-laureate—William Whitehead, who accepted that office, after Gray had refused it, in 1757. Whitehead was a native of Cambridge, being the son of the baker of Pembroke, and came to Clare from Winchester in 1735. He began his poetic work, under the patronage of Pope, while still at school, but eventually turned to the stage, acting as Garrick's adviser and writing a number of comedies himself.

One of the best known Clare dons in the eighteenth century was William Whiston, translator of Josephus, and Newton's successor in the Lucasian professorship of mathematics. Whiston, however, was tainted with Arian heresy, and suffered for it. He was expelled from his Chair and debarred from the Royal Society. In his *Memoirs* he throws some amusing lights upon the Fellows of the period; and, in particular, upon one candidate for a Fellowship who, thinking at first that the majority of the electors were " on the side of the drinkers," drank hard with them at the tavern for a month or six weeks; then, finding that he was mistaken, he " sorely repented of his debauchery and tried earnestly to recover his old friends' votes, but to no purpose."

Of the making of eighteenth-century anecdote, whether in Clare or elsewhere, there is no end; but one remarkable feature of the recent Masters of Clare may be noted—their longevity. William Webb was appointed in 1815 and died in 1856. His successor, Edward Atkinson, was Master until 1915—two Masters in a hundred years. Such are the benefits of life spent in haunts of ancient peace.

TRINITY HALL: THE LIBRARY

TRINITY HALL

the library remains, for the most part, in its original form. It was built about the end of Elizabeth's reign and the fittings completed between 1626 and 1645. Above each shelf is a sloping desk and alongside it a seat, so that the student may work either standing or sitting. The lectern habit is not widely encouraged in modern libraries, but there is no pleasanter or more convenient way of consulting a book than by resting it upon a sloping desk immediately above the shelf whence it has been taken. Some of the Trinity Hall books are still chained, though not with the chains prescribed by the founder :

"The books of the Doctors of Civil and Canon Law are to remain continuously in the said Library Chamber, fastened with iron chains for the common use of the Fellows."

From seventeenth-century conditions of study one may turn to the eighteenth-century comforts of the Combination Room, which was re-furnished about 1730. Here, on the semicircular table in front of the fire, may be seen an ingenious tramway designed to facilitate the circulation of after-dinner wine. Another element of the charm of Trinity Hall lies in the Fellows' Garden, which stretches from the Master's Lodge to the river. The mighty chestnut-trees date from the beginning of the nineteenth century, and from the raised terrace overlooking the Cam one can look down upon the punts that creep lazily to the tune of forbidden gramo-phones.

Another garden belonging to Trinity Hall has acquired a literary notoriety. It is a small triangular patch bounded by Trinity Hall Lane and two external walls of the college, and planted by Joseph Jowett, Professor of Civil Law in the University from 1782 to 1814. Jowett was described as "an elegant scholar and a man of mild and amiable

TRINITY HALL

TRINITY HALL

CLOSE to Clare—so close that in the sixteenth century it was proposed to amalgamate the two colleges— stands Trinity Hall, founded as the "College of the Scholars of the Holy Trinity of Norwich" by William Bateman, Bishop of Norwich, in 1350.

Three sides of the principal court remain on their fourteenth-century site, but originally the approach to it was through a small entrance court with two archways, a large one for carriages and a smaller one for pedestrians. These have now been removed and may be seen at the back entrance to the college in Garret Hostel Lane; and, although the buildings which formed the old entrance court remain in a reconstructed form, the college is now entered direct from the street.

The chapel was built at the end of the fourteenth century, and of the original building the walls, the buttresses, and a piscina remain. At first Trinity Hall, like Clare, held its services in the church of St John Zachary. When Henry VI swept this church away in 1445 to make room for his own magnificent college, aisles were added to St Edward's Church (a church of famous preachers, from Latimer to F. D. Maurice), one for Trinity Hall and one for Clare; as a further compensation, the advowson of St Edward's was given by the King to Trinity Hall.

From the street, the college has a somewhat gloomy aspect. Within, there is much to charm. In particular, the library remains, for the most part, in its original form. It was built about the end of Elizabeth's reign and the fittings completed between 1626 and 1645. Above each shelf is a sloping desk and alongside it a seat, so that the student may work either standing or sitting. The lectern habit is not widely encouraged in modern libraries, but there is no pleasanter or more convenient way of consulting a book than by resting it upon a sloping desk immediately above the shelf whence it has been taken. Some of the Trinity Hall books are still chained, though not with the chains prescribed by the founder :

" The books of the Doctors of Civil and Canon Law are to remain continuously in the said Library Chamber, fastened with iron chains for the common use of the Fellows."

From seventeenth-century conditions of study one may turn to the eighteenth-century comforts of the Combination Room, which was re-furnished about 1730. Here, on the semicircular table in front of the fire, may be seen an ingenious tramway designed to facilitate the circulation of after-dinner wine. Another element of the charm of Trinity Hall lies in the Fellows' Garden, which stretches from the Master's Lodge to the river. The mighty chestnut-trees date from the beginning of the nineteenth century, and from the raised terrace overlooking the Cam one can look down upon the punts that creep lazily to the tune of forbidden gramophones.

Another garden belonging to Trinity Hall has acquired a literary notoriety. It is a small triangular patch bounded by Trinity Hall Lane and two external walls of the college, and planted by Joseph Jowett, Professor of Civil Law in the University from 1782 to 1814. Jowett was described as " an elegant scholar and a man of mild and amiable

manners," but he was of small stature, and his garden provoked
a famous epigram, of which there are many variants :

> " A little garden little Jowett made
> And fenced it with a little palisade ;
> But when this little garden made a little talk
> He changed it to a little gravel walk ;
> If you would know the mind of little Jowett
> This little garden don't a little show it."

Jowett is one of the many Fellows of Trinity Hall who
have filled the Chair of Civil Law. This is but natural,
since the college was primarily designed for students of the
canon and civil law. Jowett was succeeded by J. W. Geldart
and Sir Henry Sumner Maine, of Pembroke, who was
Master of Trinity Hall from 1877 to 1888.

Other famous lawyers who have presided over the
college are Stephen Gardiner, " the great instrument of
Henry VIII," who inspired the Six Articles and became
Lord Chancellor in Mary's reign ; John Bond, who was
elected, when John Selden refused the mastership, in 1646 ;
Sir James Marriott (1764–1803), a Judge of the Admiralty
Court, who was, in his early years, a suitor for the hand of
Hester Lynch Salusbury, afterwards Mrs Thrale.

But the study of law has not been the only occupation
of Trinity Hall men. One of the early Cambridge poets,
Thomas Tusser, author of *Five Hundred Points of Good
Husbandry*, was happier at the Hall than he had been at
Eton :

> " From Paules I went, to Eaton sent,
> To learne streight waies, the latin phraies,
> Where fifty three stripes given to mee,
> At once I had :
> For fault but small, or none at all,
> It came to pass, thus beat I was,
> See Vdall see, the mercie of thee
> To me poore lad.

" From London hence, to Cambridge thence,
    With thanks to thee, O Trinitee,
    That to thy hall, so passing all,
            I got at last :
    There joy I felt, there trim I dwelt,
    There heaven from hell I shifted well,
    With learned men, a number then,
            The time I past."

In the eighteenth century the college was graced by the presence of Philip Dormer Stanhope, fourth Earl of Chesterfield. Writing in later years, Chesterfield thus described himself during his Cambridge period :

" At nineteen I left the University of Cambridge, where I was an absolute pedant : when I talked my best, I quoted Horace ; when I aimed at being facetious, I quoted Martial ; and when I had a mind to be a fine gentleman, I talked Ovid. I was convinced that none but the ancients had common sense ; that the classics contained everything that was either necessary, useful or ornamental to men, and I was not without thoughts of wearing the *toga virilis* of the Romans instead of the vulgar and illiberal dress of the moderns."

Chesterfield, whatever his qualities may have been as a letter-writer, cannot be said to rank high among Cambridge poets, but a poet of an earlier generation who may at least be partially claimed by Trinity Hall is Robert Herrick, who migrated from St John's in 1616. According to Mr Birrell, himself a Hall man, Herrick is " still reckoned very pretty reading, even by boating men."

On the whole, it is perhaps not unfair to say that the Hall has been more famous for boating men than for poets. Recently the Boat Club celebrated its centenary, and the names of many old oarsmen, now distinguished in other fields, were duly commemorated. Among the living heroes are Mr Justice Romer, Mr Reginald McKenna, and Mr Stanley Bruce, Prime Minister of Australia. To the older generation belonged Sir Leslie Stephen, who was made a Fellow and Tutor of Trinity Hall in 1854, and was " in the very first class " as a rowing coach. In his *Sketches from Cambridge* he celebrated the undying enthusiasm of the rowing man :

" We recover from the fever of our youth, but its vehemence is proved by enduring traces left behind. Who can forget the time when the fate of cabinets and armies, the expulsion of Pio Nono or the accession of Napoleon III, seemed to him of infinitely less importance than the decision of the University boat-race ? An exciting election or an important vote in the Senate sometimes fills our streets with a crowd of rarely-seen barristers and country parsons. Amongst them you recognize a pair of broad shoulders and a jovial red face ; your friend is as big as ever round the chest and a good deal bigger round the waist ; his black coat and white tie, and an indefinable air of clerical gravity, have not effectually disguised him. He tries to persuade you that he has come to save the Church, or to secure the adoption of a petition against the abolition of church-rates, or of a scheme for theological education. But, after a sentence of due wisdom, he inquires—

" ' How about the University boat ? ' "

GREAT ST. MARY'S CHURCH

GREAT ST MARY'S CHURCH

GREAT ST MARYS CHURCH

TO come out of the gate of Trinity Hall and to walk eastwards up Senate House Passage (that curious and converging alley in which bicyclists and pedestrians continue to jostle each other for the mastery) is to find oneself in the very heart of the University. To the age-long question of the foreigner : " Where is the University ? " the only answer is to take him into Senate House Yard and bid him look around. The Senate House itself was built in 1730 and is the work of James Gibbs. Undoubtedly the view of its southern façade from King's Parade is one in which Cambridge men may take a quiet pride, especially as it is a view which has more than once been threatened with obstruction. Gibbs's original design, indeed, was for a central University Library block with the Senate House projecting as a northern wing and with a similar wing on the south. This proposal was crushed by the opposition of James Burrough, Master of Caius and a prominent amateur architect of the eighteenth century. The scheme, he said, would so effectually shut out " that noble fabrick Kings-Chapell " that he wondered how the University or that College could bear it ; further, it would be so injurious to Caius that he was fully resolved not to bear it. It is a sad commentary that at the present day the view of the Senate House is marred only by the ill-chosen Gothic of Burrough's college.

Professors at University Sermons.   The architect was James Burrough, and the Throne was opened in 1754.   Here for more than a hundred years the dignitaries took their seats at sermons, and its common nickname was *Golgotha*.

In 1750 it was laid down in University regulations that " every person in statu pupillari who does not attend Saint Mary's Church the stated times of sermons shall forfeit the sum of sixpence for every offence."   Nevertheless the author of *Ten Minutes Advice to Freshmen* (1785) remarks :

" It is not reckoned fashionable to go to *St Mary's* on a Sunday—But I know no harm in going, nor that it is any reproach to a man's understanding to be seen publickly in the same place with the most dignified and respectable persons of the University."

One feature of Great St Mary's has acquired a fame beyond the confines of Cambridge—its chimes.   The " Cambridge Chimes" (often, but erroneously, called the " Westminster Chimes") were composed about 1790 by Dr Jowett, of Trinity Hall, with the assistance, perhaps, of the famous Dr Crotch.

Great St Mary's is a civic, as well as an academic, centre ; on one of the tower-buttresses may be seen a mark which is the official starting-point of distances as reckoned from Cambridge.   It was on 19th October 1732 that " a circular mark of 14 inches and an half in diameter, and about 2 foot 8 inches from ye ground, was cut on ye South-west Buttress of St Maries Steeple in Cambridge fronting the Publick Schools.   From this Buttress ye sixteen miles from Cambridge to Barkway had before been measur'd."

Behind St Mary's is the Market Place, or, more properly, Market Hill.   The name " Hill " was originally applied to any ground upon a higher level than the surrounding fen, and   though   the   old   Market   Cross   has   gone,   the   haber-

GREAT ST MARY'S CHURCH

TO come out of the gate of Trinity Hall and to walk eastwards up Senate House Passage (that curious and converging alley in which bicyclists and pedestrians continue to jostle each other for the mastery) is to find oneself in the very heart of the University. To the age-long question of the foreigner: " Where is the University ? " the only answer is to take him into Senate House Yard and bid him look around. The Senate House itself was built in 1730 and is the work of James Gibbs. Undoubtedly the view of its southern façade from King's Parade is one in which Cambridge men may take a quiet pride, especially as it is a view which has more than once been threatened with obstruction. Gibbs's original design, indeed, was for a central University Library block with the Senate House projecting as a northern wing and with a similar wing on the south. This proposal was crushed by the opposition of James Burrough, Master of Caius and a prominent amateur architect of the eighteenth century. The scheme, he said, would so effectually shut out " that noble fabrick Kings-Chapell " that he wondered how the University or that College could bear it ; further, it would be so injurious to Caius that he was fully resolved not to bear it. It is a sad commentary that at the present day the view of the Senate House is marred only by the ill-chosen Gothic of Burrough's college.

Behind the Senate House is the University Library, which may claim to be the oldest public library in the country. Certainly it possesses books which were left to the University in 1415. For many years the problem of housing more than a million books was a pressing one, but now the University, aided by a munificent grant from the Rockefeller trustees, has been able to publish its plans for a new Library to be built behind the new Clare building. By the end of 1934 it is hoped that the whole of the books will have been transferred to the new building.

Meanwhile the Library stands on the site of the old " Schools," older than the Colleges and the centre of mediæval University life ; to the old buildings large additions were made in the eighteenth and nineteenth centuries. Amongst the early treasures of the Library are the *Codex Bezæ*, the sixth-century manuscript of the Gospels and Acts of the Apostles in Greek and Latin ; a copy of Bede's *History*, written about A.D. 735 ; the *Book of Cerne*, a liturgical manuscript of the ninth century ; and a copy of Chaucer's translation of Boëthius, *De consolatione philosophiæ*, which was given to the University soon after Chaucer's death. But the greatest treasure of the University Library is its unique tradition of open access. Not only are there about half a million books on open shelves to which readers may go direct, but members of the Senate have the further privilege of borrowing not more than ten books at a time.

The Senate House is the scene of University legislation and of the conferment of degrees. When honorary degrees are given to distinguished strangers, a procession is formed under the arcade of the Library and the great ones march slowly round Senate House Yard. Thanks to the scarlet gowns of the doctors, such processions have not lost their element of the picturesque.

But it is not necessary for the observer of University custom to wait for these gala days. On any Sunday afternoon in full term a smaller, but not less impressive, procession may be seen passing from the Senate House to Great St Mary's. It is the Vice-Chancellor, preceded by the Esquire Bedells bearing their silver maces, on his way to attend the University Sermon. With him walks the Select Preacher, and behind him come the Heads of Houses, Doctors, and Professors. Nowadays it is not normally a large company, unless the preacher has more than ecclesiastical significance. But the form remains, and, if the Sunday happens also to be a Scarlet Day (that is, a day when Doctors wear their scarlet gowns) the scene has still sufficient colour to rouse a poet to utterance :

> " As I walked in Petty Cury on Trinity Day,
>   While the cuckoos in the fields did shout,
>   Right through the city stole the breath of the may,
>   And the scarlet doctors all about
>
> " Lifted up their heads to snuff at the breeze,
>   And forgot they were bound for Great St Mary's
>   To listen to a sermon from the Master of Caius,
>   And ' How balmy,' they said, ' the air is ! ' " [1]

The church of St Mary the Great, originally known as St Mary-by-the-Market, was almost entirely rebuilt at the end of the fifteenth century. The University made large contributions to the money required, but the work of building went on slowly and the tower was not finished until 1608. Unfortunately, many parts of the church—the rood-loft, the screen, the south porch, the west door—have been destroyed or replaced in later centuries. The disappearance of one eighteenth-century feature may be less regretted. This was the enormous " Throne," or gallery, erected in the chancel for the accommodation of Heads of Houses and

[1] Rose Macaulay, *The Two Blind Countries.*

Professors at University Sermons. The architect was James Burrough, and the Throne was opened in 1754. Here for more than a hundred years the dignitaries took their seats at sermons, and its common nickname was *Golgotha*.

In 1750 it was laid down in University regulations that " every person in statu pupillari who does not attend Saint Mary's Church the stated times of sermons shall forfeit the sum of sixpence for every offence." Nevertheless the author of *Ten Minutes Advice to Freshmen* (1785) remarks :

" It is not reckoned fashionable to go to *St Mary's* on a Sunday—But I know no harm in going, nor that it is any reproach to a man's understanding to be seen publickly in the same place with the most dignified and respectable persons of the University."

One feature of Great St Mary's has acquired a fame beyond the confines of Cambridge—its chimes. The " Cambridge Chimes" (often, but erroneously, called the " Westminster Chimes ") were composed about 1790 by Dr Jowett, of Trinity Hall, with the assistance, perhaps, of the famous Dr Crotch.

Great St Mary's is a civic, as well as an academic, centre ; on one of the tower-buttresses may be seen a mark which is the official starting-point of distances as reckoned from Cambridge. It was on 19th October 1732 that " a circular mark of 14 inches and an half in diameter, and about 2 foot 8 inches from ye ground, was cut on ye South-west Buttress of St Maries Steeple in Cambridge fronting the Publick Schools. From this Buttress ye sixteen miles from Cambridge to Barkway had before been measur'd."

Behind St Mary's is the Market Place, or, more properly, Market Hill. The name " Hill " was originally applied to any ground upon a higher level than the surrounding fen, and though the old Market Cross has gone, the haberdasher and the bookseller, the herbalist and the cheap-jack still ply their ancient trades. Not many years ago butter was still being sold by the yard, " for the conveniency of the college butlers cutting it into what they call sizes," and the " butter-measure" preserved in the Registry of the University is a relic of the ancient control of the Gown over the trading activities of the Town.

GONVILLE AND CAIUS COLLEGE: THE GATE OF HONOUR

GONVILLE AND CAIUS COLLEGE

GONVILLE AND CAIUS COLLEGE

NO founder of a college has been more completely overshadowed than Edmund Gonville, Rector of Terrington in the County of Norfolk, who in January 1347–8 founded a college of twenty scholars in dialectic and other sciences, to which he gave the name of the " Hall of the Annunciation of the Blessed Virgin." The Master and Fellows of this college, which came to be called Gonville Hall, were originally lodged in some tenements in what is now called Free School Lane (behind Corpus Christi College), but Gonville died in 1351, and the task of completing his design was left to William Bateman, Bishop of Norwich and founder of Trinity Hall. Bateman moved Gonville Hall to a site just opposite his own college, and " by altering the messuage of John de Cambridge and the tenements of John Goldecorne" made the north side of the college with a kitchen, a master's chamber over the gate-house, and fellows' chambers on either side. The college chapel was finished in 1393, and some fifty years later the court was completed by the building of a hall and a library on the west and students' rooms on the east.

Such was Gonville Hall, the college to which John Caius was admitted in 1529. In the *Ordo Senioritatis* (the equivalent of the modern Tripos List) for 1532–3, Caius was placed first in a list which included the names of three men who were to become bishops, and of one (Richard Jugge) who was to become Queen's Printer.

Shortly afterwards Caius became President of Physwick's Hostel (one of the several small foundations subsequently absorbed in Trinity College), and in 1539 left Cambridge for Padua, where he proceeded to the degree of Doctor of Medicine. After further European travel he returned to England to become President of the Royal College of Physicians and Physician to Edward VI and to Mary. Before long he was " taken with a desire to revisit the ancient University," and when he came there he was, like countless others since his time, " struck with the marvellous transformation which everything had undergone " :

" Faces and things, manners and dress were new. I saw new books ; I heard a new pronunciation ; the forms of teaching, learning, disputing all were new. Not to mention all the novelties about me—and they were endless—I found scarcely a soul who either knew me or was known to me."

Caius found his own college in a state of negligence and decay, and in 1557 obtained a royal licence to re-found Gonville Hall as Gonville and Caius College. The old buildings were repaired and came to be known as Gonville Court ; the number of fellowships was increased ; and a new code of statutes was drawn up. Caius also took in hand the enlargement of the college buildings, and in the design of Caius Court he was able to exercise his love of symbolism. The entrance was built in the High Street, and consisted of a simple archway with the word HUMILITATIS carved on the frieze. From this gate an avenue of trees led to a gateway tower, on which the word VIRTUTIS was inscribed, together with the legend " IO. CAIVS POSVIT SAPIENTIÆ 1567." The third gate, leading into Schools Street (now Senate House Passage), is the most famous of the three. It is the Gate of Honour through which the student was supposed to proceed to successful disputation in the Schools, and was not actually built until a few years after the death of Dr Caius in 1573. Nevertheless it is said to have been built of "squared hard stone wrought according to the very form and figure which Dr Caius in his lifetime had himself traced out for the Architect." The Gate of Honour, though now bereft of the sundial, weathercock, and pinnacles which once adorned it, remains one of the most exquisite examples of Renaissance work in Cambridge.

Great as is the honour in which the name of Dr Caius is held, his life at Cambridge was not a happy one. By temperament he was sympathetic with the ancient ways of religion. When he was elected to the Mastership in 1559, he found that many of the Fellows were fierce Puritans. Bitter quarrels ensued. The Master was denounced as a Papist, and protests were made to the University and to the Chancellor. The Master's reply was to expel several of the Fellows, even, it is said, to put one of them in the stocks. Still the disputes continued, and in 1572 the Vice-Chancellor wrote to Lord Burghley informing him that the "superstitious monuments" (vestments, albes, tunicles, stoles, mass-books) of Dr Caius were notorious, and that "it had been thought good by the whole consent of the heads of houses to burne the bookes and suche other thinges as servid most for idolatrous abuses, and to cause the rest to be defaced, which was accomplished . . . with the willing hartes as appeared of ye whole company of that house."

In the next year Caius left Cambridge, and soon afterwards he died. Characteristically, when very near his end, he paid a last visit to his college in order to give instructions for the design of his tomb. The tomb may be seen in the chapel to-day

" Upon it were afterwards carved his arms with the date of his death and the number of his years, according to the directions which he had himself given to his executors when alive. We inscribed upon it two short sentences only —*Vivit post funera virtus* and *Fui Caius.*"

Another benefactor of the college who has left a permanent memorial in Cambridge is Stephen Perse, M.D., Senior Fellow of the College, who, when he died in 1615, left money for the foundation of a " Grammar Free School " to be erected " on the garden grounds of the Friers " and on the " parcel of ground lying between the said gardens and the walnut trees in the Friers close," that is to say, on part of the site of the old Augustinian Friary behind Corpus. Here the school was duly built and gave its name to Free School Lane, where the laboratories now stand. The school itself remained upon its original site until 1890, when new buildings were erected in the Hills Road.

Perse founded new scholarships and fellowships in his old college and left money for the building of the rooms in which his beneficiaries should live rent free. Rooms were accordingly built facing St Michael's (now Trinity) Lane, but these, alas, were destroyed in 1868, when the Gate of Humility was removed to the Master's garden, and the whole front of the college was rebuilt by the " quaker-saint " whose Gothic work found such high favour in the governing bodies of more than one college in the seventies.

Historically, and traditionally, Caius is a medical college ; though its members resent the suggestion that its medical fame involves any neglect of the humanities. Certainly Fuller had occasion to remark that Dr Caius seemed " to have bequeathed a medicinal genius " into his foundation, and enumerated twenty-seven Doctors of Physic whom he

could himself remember.   One of the earliest of the great
Caius physicians was William Harvey, who in the year of
Perse's death, first publicly stated his theory of the circulation of the blood.   In modern times the tradition has been
carried on by Sir George Paget and Sir Clifford Allbutt,
both of whom held the Regius Professorship of Physic.

A distinguished Gonville man was Sir Thomas Gresham,
who was resident from 1530 to 1531, and afterwards became
the founder of the Royal Exchange and of the first English
paper-mill.

Of Caius theologians Jeremy Taylor, a native of Cambridge, is perhaps the best known.   By a most splendid
imagination, it is said, he gave " a fascination to his divinity."
In the eighteenth century Dr Samuel Clarke was a scholar
of remarkable versatility :   he edited Homer and Cæsar,
translated Newton's *Optics* into Latin, and wrote meta-
physical treatises on the Being and Attributes of God.   Like
his biographer, Whiston, however, he was an Arian.   Accordingly his name was carefully excluded from Johnson's
Dictionary, but it is noteworthy that on his death-bed
Johnson urged upon his medical attendant, Dr Brocklesby,
the study of Samuel Clarke, since he was " fullest on the
propitiatory sacrifice."

Edward Thurlow, who afterwards became Lord Chancellor and presided over the trial of Warren Hastings, matriculated as a Perse scholar of Caius in 1748, but his college
career gave no hint of future distinction.   He was idle and
unruly and was sent down without a degree.

If Caius can claim no long list of poets, it has, like Clare,
a poet-laureate in its annals.   This was Thomas Shadwell,
of whom a Cambridge historian wrote laconically that " he
was the author of seventeen dramatic pieces, of which his
Epsom Wells is said to be the most admired."   Shadwell was

engaged in a fierce literary warfare with Dryden, and it was at the Revolution that Dryden's laureateship passed to his enemy. "I do not pretend," said the Lord Chamberlain, "to say how great a poet Shadwell may be, but I am sure he is an honest man."

A more respectable Caius poet was John Hookham Frere, the translator of Aristophanes, who became a fellow of the college in 1793. Previously he had won a university prize for a Latin essay on "Whether it be allowable to hope for the improvement of morals and for the cultivation of virtue in the rising state of Botany Bay."

In the modern history of Caius there stands out prominently the name of Sir Hugh Kerr Anderson who was Master from 1912 to 1928. Of him it was said : "There is hardly any great project which has come to fruition in Cambridge for many years but he has been its most inspiring forwarder." Amongst the great projects was the new University Library in some portion of which the name of Anderson will no doubt be commemorated.

Of these worthies, and of many others, portraits are to be seen in the college to-day, but perhaps the most beautiful relic is the slender silver *caduceus* or sceptre, originally given by Dr Caius to the College of Physicians during his presidency, and afterwards transferred to the college at the time of its re-foundation. On feast nights it is still laid out upon its original silk cushion. "We give thee," said Caius, "the Cushion of Reverence. . . . We give thee the Rod of prudent Government."

TRINITY COLLEGE : THE GREAT COURT

TRINITY COLLEGE: THE GREAT GATEWAY

TRINITY COLLEGE

THE greatness of Trinity is the greatness not of accident, but of history. In 1545 an Act of Parliament was passed for the dissolution of the colleges, and the University besought Queen Katherine Parr to plead with the King on its behalf. The Queen replied first that a letter written in English, rather than in Latin, would have been " aptest for her intelligence "; secondly, that the University ought not so much to " hunger for the exquisite knowledge of profane learning " as to apply its learning to " the attaining and setting forth the better Christ's reverend and most sacred doctrine "; thirdly, that she had " attempted her lord the King's Majesty for the stablishment of the University's livelihood and possessions." So, in the last year of his reign, Henry VIII established a truly royal foundation. It was to occupy "the soil, ground, sites and precincts " of King's Hall, Michaelhouse, Physwick's Hostel, and other hostels ; it was to be a college of " literature, the sciences, philosophy, good arts, and sacred theology "; it was to consist of one master and sixty fellows and scholars ; it was to be called " Trinity College, within the town and University of Cambridge, of King Henry the Eight's foundation."

Michaelhouse and King's Hall, the nuclei of the King's foundation, had histories of their own. The first of them could, indeed, claim to be the earliest embodiment of the college system in Cambridge, since its statutes were drawn up end of the court, and for the design of this Sir Christopher Wren was probably responsible. Certainly at the other end of the court Wren produced, in the Library of Trinity, one of the masterpieces of his art. Isaac Barrow, Master of the College from 1673 to 1677, was primarily responsible for its erection. Having pressed the University to build a theatre ("very magnificent and stately, and at least exceeding that at Oxford "), and having been snubbed for his pains, " he declared that he would go straight to his college, and lay out the foundations of a building to enlarge his back court, and close it with a stately library, which should be more magnificent and costly than what he had proposed to them."

The outcome was the noble building which is as notable for its massive river-front as for its harmony with the rest of Nevile's Court. Wren designed not only the building itself, but the shelves, tables, and chairs which it was to contain. " We are scrupulous in small matters," he wrote, " and you must pardon us ; the Architects are as great pedants as Criticks or Heralds."

The carving of the bookshelves was done by Grinling Gibbons, and the treasures of the library (first folios of Shakespeare, manuscripts of Milton, Tennyson and many others) are worthy of their setting.

Nevile's Court has seen many strange sights : Byron lived there and climbed on to the library roof by night ; in the northern cloister Newton, by timing the echo, is said to have first calculated the velocity of sound ; when Edward VII (then Prince of Wales) brought his bride to Cambridge in 1864, the whole court was covered and made into a ballroom ; nearly sixty years later his grandson, the present Prince of Wales, sat on the terrace and watched a display of folk-dancing ; but the most remarkable use to which the court was ever put was in September 1914, when it became for a

TRINITY COLLEGE: THE HALL FROM NEVILE'S COURT

time the First Eastern General Hospital and was filled with soldiers wounded at Mons or at the Aisne.

Trinity, of course, has other buildings besides those contained in its two most famous courts. There is Bishop's Hostel, built in 1670; New Court, built in the Gothic manner characteristic of Wilkins; and Whewell's Courts, the gloomiest in Cambridge, on the other side of Trinity Street. The great size and wealth of Trinity have made it one of the greatest of all the training-grounds of famous men. If, for instance, the traveller turns to the right immediately after entering the Great Court, as the guide-books instruct him, he will come to a staircase associated with the names of Newton, Macaulay, and Thackeray. Of Newton's way of life in Trinity his kinsman, Humphrey Newton, wrote:

"He very seldom sat by the fire in his chamber excepting y^t long frosty winter [1683–4], which made him creep to it against his will. I can't say I ever saw him wear a night gown, but his wearing clothes that he put off at night, at night do I say, yea rather towards ye morning, he put on again at his rising. He never slept in ye day-time y^t I ever perceived; I believe he grudged ye short time he spent in eating and sleeping. . . . He kept neither dog nor cat in his chamber, wch made well for ye old woman his bedmaker, she faring much ye better for it, for in a morning she has sometimes found both dinner and supper scarcely tasted of, wch ye old woman has very pleasantly and mumpingly gone away with."

Macaulay was devoted to his college and intensely proud of his fellowship. His nephew has given a graphic picture of its delights and privileges:

"I can never remember the time when it was not diligently impressed upon me that, if I minded my syntax, I might eventually hope to reach a position which would give me three hundred pounds a year; a stable for my horse, six dozen of audit ale every Christmas, a loaf and two pats of butter every morning, and a good dinner for nothing, with as many almonds and raisins as I could eat at dessert."

If, again following the instructions of the guide-book, the traveller enters the ante-chapel, he will find statues of Bacon, Barrow, Whewell, and Tennyson, as well as of Newton and Macaulay. It was a poet of another college who immortalised this ante-chapel and the restored gateway of Edward III alongside it :

> " Near me hung Trinity's loquacious clock,
> Who never let the quarters, night or day,
> Slip by him unproclaimed, and told the hours
> Twice over with a male and female voice.
> Her pealing organ was my neighbour too ;
> And from my pillow, looking forth by light
> Of moon or favouring stars, I could behold
> The antechapel where the statue stood
> Of Newton with his prism and silent face,
> The marble index of a mind for ever
> Voyaging through strange seas of thought alone." [1]

Trinity, of course, has its own long roll of poets. In the seventeenth century it claimed Dryden, Marvell, Herbert, Randolph, and Cowley. Of Dryden's undergraduate career not much is known save that he was "discommuned for contumacy to the Vice-Master." George Herbert, on the other hand, became a Fellow in 1616 and Public Orator a few years later ; according to Walton he performed the functions of that office " with as becoming and grave a gaiety, as any had ever before or since his time ; for he had acquired great learning, and was blessed with a high fancy, a civil and sharp wit, and with a natural elegance, both in his behaviour, his tongue, and his pen." Thomas Randolph celebrated, among other characters, " the Cambridge dun" :

[1] Wordsworth, *The Prelude*.

TRINITY COLLEGE: THE HALL

> " What damage given to my doors might be,
>   If doors might actions have of battery !
>   And when they find their coming to no end,
>   They dun by proxy, and their letters send . . ."

Cowley commemorated his love of Cambridge and Trinity in a Latin poem, written after his ejection in 1643 :

> " O mihi jucundum *Grantæ* super omnia *Nomen !*
>   O penitus toto corde receptus *Amor !* . . .
>   O cara ante alias, magnorum nomine *Regum*
>   Digna *Domus ! Trini* nomine digna *Dei !* "

As Cowley wrote on the death of his friend, William Hervey :

> " Ye fields of *Cambridge*, our dear *Cambridge*, say
>   Have ye not seen us walking every day ? "

so Tennyson, in a more famous poem, commemorated his friend, Arthur Hallam :

> " The same gray flats again, and felt
>   The same, but not the same ; and last
>   Up that long walk of limes I past
>   To see the rooms in which he dwelt.

> " Another name was on the door :
>   I linger'd : all within was noise
>   Of songs, and clapping hands, and boys
>   That crash'd the glass and beat the floor."

Hallam's rooms were in New Court, and, in themselves, are less worthy of poetic immortality than is the " long walk of limes " which was planted in 1672 and leads to the Trinity bridge.

Portraits of many more of the famous men of Trinity may be seen in the hall, where the place of honour is naturally given to Henry VIII. In a less conspicuous place is Queen Mary, who was also a benefactress of the college. A visitor once commented on the superior position of Henry VIII's portrait. " It is better," was the reply, " to marry than to burn."

In the library, too, there is a famous series of busts, the work of the eighteenth-century sculptor, Roubiliac. Among them is a bust of Richard Bentley, of St John's, the

12

most famous classical scholar of the eighteenth century and Master of Trinity from 1699 to 1742. Never has there been a stormier reign in Trinity or in any other college. Throughout the period there was war between the Master and Fellows. In 1710 the Fellows appealed to the Bishop of Ely:

"Why," they asked of the Master, "did you of your own Head pull down a good Stair-case in your Lodge, and give Orders and Directions for building a new one, and that too fine for common Use?

"Why did you use scurrilous Words and Language to several of the Fellows, particularly by calling Mr *Eden* an Ass, and Mr *Rashly* the College Dog, and by telling Mr *Cock* he would die in his Shoes?"

The story of Bentley's career is too long to be told here. For a time he was deprived of his degrees; further, he was found guilty in the Bishop's Court of violating the College statutes, and was sentenced to be deprived of his Mastership. The agent of deprivation was the Vice-Master, who shortly resigned his office. His successor was a stout friend of Bentley. Great efforts were made to force the new Vice-Master to act, but without success; Bentley remained at the Lodge. At another time Bentley was summoned to give evidence in the Vice-Chancellor's Court in connection with a suit for libel. There was a certain difficulty in serving the writ: "The Esquire-beadles . . . were all as averse to such perilous service, as the mice in the fable were to undertake the office of belling the cat." However, one of the beadles was bribed with a double fee. Bentley gave the officers no trouble, but arranged to be on duty as court chaplain at St James's at the date fixed for the trial. The proceedings against him were abandoned. When the Regius Professorship of Divinity fell vacant in 1717, Bentley was a strong candidate on the grounds of scholarship, but was bitterly opposed. One of

the seven electors was the Vice-Chancellor. It was arranged
that about the time of the election he should be absent from
Cambridge, and that he should appoint Bentley as his Deputy.
Bentley was elected by four votes to three, one of the voters
being the Deputy Vice-Chancellor.

A few incidents of this kind illustrate the difference
between the methods of eighteenth-century academic controversy and those of to-day. Even in recent years questions
such as those of Women's Degrees and Compulsory Greek
have produced continuous showers of contending " fly-
sheets " ; but it is a far cry from the decorous phrasing of
these modern manifestoes to such epithets as " mountebank,"
" maggot," " gnawing-rat," and " cabbage-head," which
formed part of the controversial vocabulary of the age of
Bentley.

But, in the matter of scholarship, the Bentley tradition
in the Mastership of Trinity has been maintained. In the
nineteenth century Whewell, W. H. Thompson, and H. M.
Butler filled the office, and the Master of Trinity is traditionally not only a scholar, but an omniscient scholar.
Stories of his ability to talk learnedly on any subject from
Chinese metaphysic to leg-break bowling are current in
every generation of undergraduates.

Trinity is in size *sui generis*, and what it gains in greatness it loses perhaps in homeliness. But not the least of
its charms is the bowling-green, laid out in the middle of
the seventeenth century and now hidden away behind the
north-west corner of the Great Court. It is part of the
old garden of King's Hall, and the range at the eastern end
is one of the few fragments that survive of that earlier
college which was absorbed into the lordly foundation of
Henry VIII.

ST. JOHN'S COLLEGE: THE BRIDGES

ST JOHN'S COLLEGE

ST JOHN'S COLLEGE

A LITTLE way past the Great Gate of Trinity stands another noble gateway—that of St John's. Though it is not, strictly speaking, the entrance to another royal foundation, it commemorates a lady who, at her death in 1509, " had thirty kings and queens allied to her within the fourth degree either of blood or affinity." This was Margaret Beaufort, Countess of Richmond, and mother of Henry VII, and on the entrance gateway may be seen " the lions of England, the lilies of France, the antelopes of the sixth Henry, the portcullis of the house of Beaufort, the Tudor rose, the plumes of the Plantagenets, and the *marguérites* of the foundress herself."

Nearly four hundred years before the actual foundation of the college (1511), a Hospital of the Brethren of St John the Evangelist had been established under the rule of a community of Augustinian Canons. It was to this community that Hugh de Balsham introduced a number of secular scholars, who were eventually removed to the other end of the High Street to become the nucleus of the first Cambridge college. Meanwhile the Hospital of St John continued to grow and flourish until the end of the fifteenth century. Then decay set in, owing to the misgovernment of the Master, and the house was dissolved by a papal bull in 1510.

Some years before this the Lady Margaret had, at the instigation of her confessor, John Fisher, become the patroness of Cambridge learning and had founded a Professorship of Divinity. As Chancellor, Fisher had welcomed his patroness when she visited Cambridge in 1506, and, just before her death, he persuaded her to endow a new college upon the site of the moribund Hospital. Fisher himself and Richard Fox, Bishop of Winchester, were two of the eight executors entrusted with the completion of the project.

Work upon the new buildings was begun in 1511, and the first court was upon much the same plan, and in much the same style, as that of Queens'. The north side of the court, however, containing the chapel and the master's lodging, was destroyed in 1869 to make way for a more elaborate chapel designed by Sir Gilbert Scott—a building which would look well enough as a parish church, but will never accord with Renaissance brickwork. On the opposite side of the court the brickwork has also been spoiled, and the heavy hand of Essex has left its mark in the form of a facing of unlovely stone and the fitting of sash windows. A fine gateway, richly adorned with the emblems of Tudor heraldry and with a statue of St John, leads through the screens into the Second Court, one of the most beautiful in Cambridge. It was built of brick at the end of the sixteenth century, largely at the expense of Lady Mary Cavendish, Countess of Shrewsbury, whose arms may be seen over the western gate. It is a famous court, and the whole of the upper floor of its northern side is occupied by a yet more famous room—the Combination Room, which was originally the Master's Gallery. It is nearly 100 feet in length, with panelled walls and a low, richly-decorated plaster ceiling. The room is beautiful at any time, but if it is to be seen in its full glory, it must be seen in candle-light quietly reflected in smoothly-gleaming mahogany and in lustrous silver plate. About 1624 the Library (a "curious example of Jacobean Gothic") was

ST. JOHN'S COLLEGE: A CORNER OF THE SECOND COURT

built in continuation of the northern side of the Second
Court. The beautiful oriel window in its western wall over-
looks the river, and alongside may be seen the initials of the
benefactor responsible for the building—I.L.C.S. (Joannes
Lincolniensis Custos Sigilli).[1] Inside, the original bookcases
of dark oak remain, though most of the smaller cases have
been heightened, with the result that the sloping desks
are rendered useless. The ends of the cases are panelled,
and, according to mediæval custom, a small folding cupboard
discloses a catalogue of the books originally contained in
the particular case.

The library and the western range of the Second Court
formed two sides of a third court, which was completed in
the style of Wren, and possibly from designs by his pupil,
Hawksmoor, in 1671. The stone bridge, now known as the
Old Bridge, was built in 1696 by Robert Grumbold, though
he was probably not responsible for the design. More famous
amongst sightseers and photographers is the " Bridge of
Sighs," which leads from the Third Court to the new buildings
on the other side of the river. When, in 1825, it was decided
that the college needed more rooms for its undergraduates,
it was agreed " that it be an instruction to the Architects
[Rickman and Hutchinson] to follow as nearly as may be the
style of the present Second Court, with such Improvements
as the Architect may suggest." Two years later, it was still
intended to build the new court of brick, but the passion for
Gothic was too strong, and the Perpendicular style was
chosen. The same style was naturally adopted for the
bridge to link the new with the old ; but disciplinary as well
as architectural factors had to be taken into account :

" An ingeniously contrived bridge, whose passage is
roofed, and enclosed at the sides by open tracery, forms the

[1] John Williams, Bishop of Lincoln and Keeper of the Great Seal.

13

communication from the older quadrangles. By this device the nocturnal inclosure of the students within the walls is preserved without interfering with free communication between the courts."

In its early years, St John's was the greatest college in Cambridge, and, until late in the eighteenth century, it was doubtful whether Trinity or St John's would take precedence in the matter of numbers. To-day Trinity has no competitors in size, but in the sixteenth century Roger Ascham, the Renaissance scholar who was made a Fellow of St John's in 1534, could boast that " Trinity College . . . at the first erection was but *colonia deducta* out of St John's, not only for their master, fellows and scholars, but also (which is more) for their whole both order of learning and discipline of manners." Similarly Thomas Nash, who entered the college in 1582, described it as " a university within itself, shining so far above all other houses, halls and hospitals whatever, that no college in the town was able to compare with the tithe of her students." Robert Greene, the dramatist, was also a member of St John's, but took his Master's degree from Clare, and Harvey censured his " fonde disguisinge of a master of arte with ruffianly haire." Ben Jonson, who described himself as " Master of Arts of both Universities, by their favour, not his study," is assigned by John Aubrey to Trinity, and by Thomas Fuller to St John's ; actually there is no evidence of his residence at either college.

Statesmen, as well as poets, flourished at St John's in the sixteenth century. William Cecil, Lord Burghley, and Sir Thomas Wyatt both had their education there—Cecil, " of well-balanced and weighty remark," and Wyatt, " of lively, but pertinent wit." Thomas Howard, too, was there (" Then sware Lord Thomas Howard : ' Fore God I am no coward ' "), and Henry Wriothesley, Earl of Southampton, the patron of

ST. JOHN'S COLLEGE: THE LIBRARY

Shakespeare and other poets. A later Johnian statesman, less fortunate than Burghley in his service to his monarch, was Thomas Wentworth, Earl of Strafford.

Matthew Prior came up to St John's in 1683 and quickly displayed his facility of versification in more than one poem written in celebration of the Lady Foundress :

> " Hail mighty Patroness ! Hail great and Good !
> Hail doubly fam'd for Virtue and for blood !
> Hail Thou, whose Acts shou'd I presume to show
> I shou'd blasphem by Epithete too low.
> Hail St or Princess royal or Divine,
> Hail wonder of our Sex and Fame of Thine
> Be Thou my Muse vouchsafe to look on me
> The meanest of thy learnèd Progeny
> Inspire my Soul that I may sing Thy fame
> And raise a work eternal as my Theam
> Inspire my Soul that I may loudly tell
> How far Thou dost all Woman kind Excell."

But all other Johnian poets are, of course, overshadowed by William Wordsworth, who entered the college in 1787 and in *The Prelude* left a record of his impressions of Cambridge in familiar lines :

> " To myself I seemed
> A man of business and expense, and went
> From shop to shop about my own affairs,
> To Tutor or to Tailor, as befel,
> From street to street with loose and careless mind.

> " I was the Dreamer, they the Dream ; I roamed
> Delighted through the motley spectacle ;
> Gowns grave, or gaudy, doctors, students, streets,
> Courts, cloisters, flocks of churches, gateways, towers :
> Migration strange for a stripling of the hills,
> A northern villager."

But the stripling soon fell into the way of ordinary under-graduate life :

> " We sauntered, played, or rioted ; we talked
> Unprofitable talk at morning hours ;
> Drifted about along the streets and walks,
> Read lazily in trivial books, went forth

To gallop through the country in blind zeal
Of senseless horsemanship, or on the breast
Of Cam sailed boisterously, and let the stars
Come forth, perhaps without one quiet thought.

" Such was the tenour of the second act
In this new life.   Imagination slept,
And yet not utterly.   I could not print
Ground where the grass had yielded to the steps
Of generations of illustrious men,
Unmoved . . ."

Lord Palmerston came up to St John's in 1803, and left it on record that the knowledge acquired by reading for half-yearly examinations was worth nothing, but that the habit of mind acquired by preparing for them was highly useful.

Many famous mathematicians came from St John's in the early part of the nineteenth century—Sir John Herschel, J. C. Adams (the discoverer of Neptune, who migrated to Pembroke), J. J. Sylvester, and Isaac Todhunter.

Nor was classical scholarship neglected. Samuel Butler, the famous Headmaster of Shrewsbury, was succeeded by another Johnian, Benjamin Hall Kennedy, who, after thirty years at Shrewsbury, returned to Cambridge to become Professor of Greek.

Samuel Butler's grandson, the author of *Erewhon*, took his degree from St John's in 1858. He steered the Lady Margaret boat when it was head of the river, and an undergraduate skit of his, entitled *The Shield of Achilles*, contains a fragmentary description of Cambridge in the manner of a literal translation of Homer :

" And in it he placed the Cam, and many boats equally rowed on both sides were going up and down on the bosom of the deep-rolling river, and the coxswains were cheering on the men, for they were going to enter the contest of the scratched fours, and three men were rowing together in a boat, strong and stout, and determined in their hearts that they would either first break a blood-vessel or earn for themselves the electro-plated-Birmingham-manufactured-magnificence of a pewter to stand on their hall tables in memorial of their strength, and from time to time drink from it the exhilarating streams of beer whensoever their dear heart should compel them. . . ."

The series of chapters in *The Way of All Flesh*, which deals with Ernest Pontifex's Cambridge career, is largely concerned with the activities of the Simeonites, but Butler was no doubt speaking from his own experience when he said that Cambridge was " the first place where he had ever been consciously and continuously happy," and many a freshman, whether at St John's or elsewhere, has felt as Butler did when he wrote :

" How can any boy fail to feel an ecstasy of pleasure on first finding himself in rooms which he knows for the next few years are to be his castle ? Here he will not be compelled to turn out of the most comfortable place as soon as he has ensconced himself in it. . . . The most cosy chair here is for himself, there is no one even to share the room with him, or to interfere with his doing as he likes in it—smoking included. Why, if such a room looked out both back and front on to a blank dead wall it would still be a paradise, how much more then when the view is of some quiet grassy court or cloister or garden, as from the windows of the greater number of rooms at Oxford and Cambridge."

MAGDALENE COLLEGE: THE PEPYSIAN LIBRARY

MAGDALENE COLLEGE

MAGDALENE COLLEGE

AS he leaves St John's, the traveller, having come to the end of the old High Street,[1] finds himself in the street which leads down to what is now called Magdalene Bridge, but what was once the Great Bridge, the bridge which appears on the first Seal of the Borough in 1423, the only bridge which has given its name to an English county.

On the right, immediately beyond the bridge, is Magdalene College, which stands on the site of Buckingham College, a hostel for Benedictine monks, established in 1428, and dissolved, with its superior house, Croyland Abbey, in 1539. Three years later it was "re-founded, under the new dedication of St Mary Magdalene, by Thomas Lord Audley of Walden, to whom the King had granted it for the purpose"; until very recently the Mastership remained in the gift of the holder of the Barony of Braybrooke as representing the Founder. The extent of Buckingham College was that of the present First Court of the college. The chapel, or at least part of it, remains as it was in 1475; the Hall was built in 1519; other portions of the court have been re-built.

A more famous building is that which forms the back of the Second Court, and commemorates the best known of all Magdalene men—Samuel Pepys. Not much is known of

---

[1] It has now four sectional names—Trumpington Street, King's Parade, Trinity Street, St John's Street.

14   105

Pepys's college career : he records himself that he " did put on his gown first " on 5th March 1650–1 ; shortly afterwards he was elected to a Spendluffe scholarship, and two years later to one on Dr Smith's foundation. Not long after this (21st October 1653) the Registrar of the college recorded that " Peapys and Hind were solemnly admonished by myself and Mr Hill, for having been scandalously over-served with drink yᵉ night before." In later years Pepys was, of course, a frequent visitor to Cambridge, and the *Diary* has many references to Magdalene men. On 25th May 1668 he took his boy and two brothers to his old college :

" And there into the butterys, as a stranger, and there drank my belly full of their beer, which pleased me, as the best I ever drank: and hear by the butler's man, who was son to Goody Mulliner over against the College, that we used to buy stewed prunes of, concerning the College and persons in it ; and find very few, only Mr Hollins and Pechell, I think, that were of my time. But I was mightily pleased to come in this condition to see and ask, and thence, giving the fellow something, away walked to Chesterton, to see our old walk, and there into the Church, the bells ringing, and saw the place I used to sit in, and so to the ferry, and ferried over to the other side, and walked with great pleasure, the river being mighty high by Barnewell Abbey : and so by Jesus College to the town, and so to our quarters, and to supper, and then to bed, being very weary and sleepy and mightily pleased with this night's walk."

Pepys was also mightily pleased on 24th August 1666 when his " new presses " for his books were brought home to him, and he spent a happy day in the furnishing of his " new closett," and in arranging his maps and pictures and books to his " most extraordinary satisfaction."

Pepys made his nephew, John Jackson, his heir ; but

since he could not be sure that Jackson's successors could be trusted to preserve his library properly, he provided in his will that after his nephew's death his books should go either to Trinity or to Magdalene, and preferably to his own college ; that, if they should go to Magdalene, they should be housed " in the new building there " ; that the library should be " continued in its present form," and should be known as the " Bibliotheca Pepysiana " ; that no books in this library should be moved except to the Master's lodge, and then not more than ten at a time ; that Trinity and Magdalene should have " a reciprocal check upon one another, the college in possession of the library being subject to an annual visitation from the other."

When Jackson died in 1723, the books and the book-cases were moved to Magdalene, and there they remain to-day. Pepys's desire that " all possible provision should be made for [his library's] unalterable preservation and perpetual security " has been fulfilled, and few bookmen have so success-fully contrived that " the infinite pains and time and cost employed in collecting and methodising " should not be wasted.

The twelve cases, or " presses," are of red oak and are fitted with glass doors. At first sight, all the books in a shelf appear to be of the same height, but this is due to Pepys's care in having little pedestals made for the smaller books, and also in having them shaped and painted to look like parts of the books themselves.

The famous *Diary* forms part of the library, and is con-tained in six quarto volumes. It remained wrapped in the obscurity of its shorthand until 1819, when John Smith, an undergraduate of St John's, was employed to decipher it. The work occupied three years, and the *Diary* was first published, in an incomplete form, in 1825. The complete edition did not appear until 1893.

One of the most notable Masters of Magdalene in the early eighteenth century was Daniel Waterland, a friend of Bentley, and a prominent writer on theological subjects. He was a man of strict economy, and the undergraduates of his time complained bitterly of the smallness of the Magdalene loaf. Very different was Thomas Chapman, Master from 1746 to 1760. He was described as " conceited and overbearing " in his rule, and Gray makes several references to him in his letters :

" Our friend Dr Chapman," he wrote on 12th August 1760, " is not expected here again in a hurry. He is gone to his grave with five fine mackerel (large and full of roe) in his belly. He eat them all at one dinner ; but his fate was a turbot on Trinity Sunday, of which he left little for the company besides bones. He had not been hearty all the week ; but after this sixth fish he never held up his head more. . . . They say he made a very good end."

Charles Kingsley came up to Magdalene in 1838, and used to climb over the old walls of the second court at an early hour in order to go fishing. He also took lessons in boxing from a negro pugilist and rode out to listen to Sedgwick's geological lectures. He was disappointed at not being elected to a Fellowship, but came back to Cambridge in 1860 as Professor of Modern History.

Charles Stewart Parnell had rooms in the Pepys building, but his career at Cambridge was undistinguished, and he left Magdalene without having taken a degree.

In 1925 there died the most famous of recent Masters of Magdalene—Arthur Christopher Benson. Few college dons have gained so wide a public, and many a tourist is as eager to see " the College Window " as " Milton's Mulberry-tree," and other show-pieces. About half-a-million people, as he noted in his *Diary*, must have been interested in what Arthur Benson said in his books; yet his writings, apparently so intimate, did not, as many of his friends have hastened to explain, reveal the man—especially the man who, in his own words, was "sustained by a quite unreasonable cheerfulness and enjoyment of life."

Magdalene, like many other colleges, has been forced to extend its buildings to the other side of the street in which it stands, but only a part of the spacious new court is as yet completed. The buildings already erected commemorate the names of Benson and of George Mallory who died on Mount Everest.

JESUS COLLEGE

JESUS COLLEGE

LEAVING Magdalene and re-crossing the bridge, the traveller may walk up Bridge Street, past the "Round Church" (one of the four English churches built in imitation of the Holy Sepulchre), past the entrance to the Union, past the site of "The Hoop," where Wordsworth alighted, and come to Jesus Lane. Turning down it, he will reach one of the most isolated and most beautiful of Cambridge colleges. Like many other colleges, Jesus replaced an earlier religious foundation, the Priory of St Radegund ; but unlike every other college, its buildings preserve the plan, not of the English country-house, but of the mediæval monastery.

The Priory of St Radegund was in existence early in the twelfth century, and consisted of a large cruciform church with a central tower, a chapter-house, cloisters, refectory, dormitory, and kitchen. The record of a visitation made in 1373 shows that the nuns " were not living in perfect peace and harmony, and that the roofs did not keep out the rain."

By 1496 matters had gone from bad to worse, and John Alcock, Bishop of Ely, found in his visitation that, by the negligence and dissolute disposition of the Prioress and the nuns, the whole House had fallen into a state of dilapidation and decay. The Bishop therefore petitioned the King for a licence to found a college in its place. Accordingly in 1497 Jesus College (called for a very short time " The College of

S. Mary the Virgin, S. John the Evangelist, and S. Rade-gund ") was founded by royal charter. The church of the nuns was too large for a college consisting of a Master, six Fellows, and a certain number of scholars, and the aisles were therefore pulled down, together with four bays at the end of the nave. The cloisters were altered, and the arches of the chapter-house walled up. The hall was partially re-built, but still stands on the site of the old refectory. Beneath it are the cellars, this arrangement being essentially a monastic, not a collegiate, feature.

Amongst the unique features of Jesus is the " Chimney," the high walled path which leads from the road to the entrance gateway. Here is yet another example of the brick-work which is the pride of Cambridge. In the centre of the gate-way is a statue of the founder, together with his punning crest, a cock standing on a globe. The restoration of the chapel was begun in 1846. Fragments of thirteenth-century lancet windows were found in the east wall. These gave the key to the general design, and the windows were filled with glass designed by Pugin. More famous are the windows in the transepts and nave (now the ante-chapel), which were put up in the seventies from designs by Morris, Madox Brown, and Burne-Jones.

Apart from its special interest in displaying the monastic plan, Jesus is almost uniquely fortunate in standing comfort-ably in its own grounds. No shops, or streets, or houses press upon its borders, and behind the college is the Grove con-taining the college playing-fields. A ditch separates the Grove from Midsummer Common, and beyond the Common is the river with its line of college boat-houses. The Jesus boat-house has a special distinction—a clock-tower which com-memorates the college's headship of the river from 1875 to 1885.

Amongst the early alumni of Jesus, the most famous is Thomas Cranmer, who came to the college at the age of fourteen in 1503. As an undergraduate he formed no high opinion of the tuition he received:

"The scholar of such an one I was," he wrote, "who when he came to any hard chapter, which he well understood not, would find some pretty toy to shift it off, and to skip over to another chapter, of which he could better skill."

Cranmer became a Fellow about 1511, and shortly afterwards married one Joan, who was living at the Dolphin Inn in Bridge Street. This meant the resignation of his Fellowship, and Cranmer appears to have lived for a time at the Dolphin and to have given lectures at what was then the Benedictine foundation of Buckingham College. A year later, however, his wife died, and Cranmer was re-elected a Fellow of Jesus on the ground of his "towardlinesse in learning."

Fulke Greville, "Servant to Queen Elizabeth, Conceller to King James, Frend to Sir Philip Sidney," came up to Jesus in 1568, and at his death founded a history lectureship in the University. The endowment, however, was lost in the troublous times of the Civil War.

One of the greatest of the Masters of Jesus also suffered much in the Civil War. This was Richard Sterne, previously a scholar of Trinity, who was made Master in 1633. He did a great deal for the reform of the college finance, but his work was interrupted by appeals from King Charles for money and plate. Jesus, like most other colleges, responded to the appeal, and the Master afterwards paid the penalty:

"Together with Dr Beale, Master of St John's, and Dr Martin, Master of Queens', he was seized by Cromwell (who had with some Parties of Soldiers surrounded the several Chapels, whilst the Scholars were at Prayers) and carried in Triumph to London."

After the Restoration Sterne became Archbishop of York, and in 1735 his great-grandson, Laurence Sterne, matriculated from Jesus.   Very little is known of the novelist's undergraduate career, save that he got into debt and formed a friendship with John Hall, the Eugenius of *Tristram Shandy*. College tradition associated this friendship with a walnut-tree, cut down about the end of the eighteenth century, under which one of the two is alleged to have written :

> " This shou'd be the Tree of Knowledge,
>   As it stands in so very wise a Colledge."

Samuel Taylor Coleridge came up to Jesus in 1791. " What evenings," wrote a contemporary, " have I spent in those [*i.e.* Coleridge's] rooms ! What little suppers, or sizings, as they were called, have I enjoyed when Æschylus and Plato and Thucydides were pushed aside with a pile of lexicons etc., to discuss the pamphlets of the day.   Ever and anon a pamphlet issued from the pen of Burke.   There was no need of having the book before us.   Coleridge had read it in the morning, and in the evening he would repeat whole pages *verbatim*.   Frend's trial was then in progress.   Pamphlets swarmed from the press.   Coleridge had read them all ; and in the evening, with our negus, we had them *viva-voce* gloriously."

" Frend's trial " has reference to the man celebrated by Charles Lamb :

> " Friend of the friendless, friend of all mankind,
>   To thy wide friendships I have not been blind ;
>   But looking at them nearly, in the end
>   I love thee most that thou art Dyer's Frend."

William Frend, of Christ's, had migrated to Jesus, and was Rector of St Michael's, Longstanton.   Having became a Unitarian, he was deprived of his Fellowship at Jesus, and was prosecuted in the Vice-Chancellor's court for Republican opinions in 1793.   Undergraduate opinion ran strongly in

JESUS COLLEGE: THE GATEWAY

Frend's favour, and one of the loudest interrupters in the gallery of the Senate House was Coleridge, though another undergraduate—one Charnock, of Clare—bore the brunt of the Proctor's anger. Coleridge, according to Gunning, affected a peculiar style of conversation :

" Speaking of the dinners in Hall, he described the veal which was served up to them (and which was large and coarse) in the following words :—' We have veal, Sir, tottering on the verge of beef ! ' "

Coleridge, like Sterne, became involved in debts, and in 1793 enlisted in the 15th Dragoons under the name of Silas Tomkins Comberbacke. But in a few months he was back at Jesus. He was admonished by the Master, and set to translate the works of Demetrius Phalerus into English. In the next year, 1794, he again became restless. Pantisocracy filled his head, and his drama, entitled *The Fall of Robespierre*, again brought him into conflict with the authorities. In an inauspicious hour, as he afterwards wrote, he left the " friendly cloisters and happy grove of quiet, ever honoured Jesus College, Cambridge."

Frend's favour, and one of the loudest interrupters in the gallery of the Senate House was Coleridge, though another undergraduate—one Charnock, of Clare—bore the brunt of the Proctor's anger. Coleridge, according to Gunning, affected a peculiar style of conversation :

" Speaking of the dinners in Hall, he described the veal which was served up to them (and which was large and coarse) in the following words :—' We have veal, Sir, tottering on the verge of beef ! ' "

Coleridge, like Sterne, became involved in debts, and in 1793 enlisted in the 15th Dragoons under the name of Silas Tomkins Comberbacke. But in a few months he was back at Jesus. He was admonished by the Master, and set to translate the works of Demetrius Phalerus into English. In the next year, 1794, he again became restless. Pantisocracy filled his head, and his drama, entitled *The Fall of Robespierre*, again brought him into conflict with the authorities. In an inauspicious hour, as he afterwards wrote, he left the " friendly cloisters and happy grove of quiet, ever honoured Jesus College, Cambridge."

SIDNEY SUSSEX COLLEGE—CHRIST'S COLLEGE

CHRIST'S COLLEGE: THE GATEWAY

BEHIND the high wall at the corner of Jesus Lane and Bridge Street are the gardens of Sidney Sussex, the college which stands on the site of a house of Franciscan Friars dissolved in 1538. The foundress was the Lady Frances, daughter of Sir William Sidney and widow of the second Earl of Sussex. By 1596, when the building of the new college was begun, everything of the old Franciscan house had been destroyed, save the Refectory. The architect of the new college was Ralph Symons, builder of the second court of St John's and of the hall of Trinity. The First Court of Sidney Sussex was originally of brick, but was largely rebuilt in the eighteenth and nineteenth centuries. The old Refectory of the Friars served for many years as a chapel, but was destroyed and replaced by a building designed by Essex in 1780. Quite recently the Chapel has been enlarged, and it is now one of the most interesting pieces of modern architecture in Cambridge. It is wholly Renaissance in character; the walls are panelled in oak, which displays a profusion of carving; the pavement is of elaborate marble, and the whole building has a remarkable and, perhaps, a slightly un-English individuality.

Of the college career of the greatest of the alumni of Sidney—Oliver Cromwell—very little is known. He was entered as a fellow-commoner on the day of Shakespeare's death, 23rd April 1616. He is said to have been

modern part, built without the quadrangle towards the
gardens, of exact architecture." One set of rooms in this
building contains some of the best panelling in Cambridge.

Perhaps the gardens of Christ's are more famous than its
buildings, and chiefly because, as Dyer says:

" Travellers are here shewn a rich mulberry tree broken
down with age, but not deserted, it being propt up with
wonderful assiduity and skill, and not merely consecrated to
Milton, but planted, we are told, with his own hand. Whether
true or not, the fancy may be improved by supposing that
Milton here meditated some of his juvenile poems, many of
them, particularly his Latin Elegies, having been written by
him while a student of this college, and relating to Cambridge."

What was told to travellers more than a hundred years
ago is still told to-day, but the Higher Critics of Cantabrigian
history assert that " Milton's Mulberry-tree " is probably the
last of a number of such trees bought in 1609. Milton was
admitted to Christ's in 1625, and, according to Aubrey's
gossip, suffered the indignity of being flogged for some breach
of college discipline. This, again, is probably apocryphal,
though flogging was not unknown as an undergraduate
punishment in the seventeenth century. In later years Milton
wrote, " with all grateful mind," of " that more than ordinary
respect which I found, above many of my equals, at the hands
of those courteous and learned men, the Fellows of that
college wherein I spent some years ; who, at my parting
after I had taken two degrees, as the manner is, signified
many ways how much better it would content them that I
would stay. . . ."

Milton left Cambridge, after taking his M.A. degree, in
1632. Of the poems of Milton which are associated with
Cambridge, the most famous, of course, is *Lycidas*. Edward

BEHIND the high wall at the corner of Jesus Lane and Bridge Street are the gardens of Sidney Sussex, the college which stands on the site of a house of Franciscan Friars dissolved in 1538. The foundress was the Lady Frances, daughter of Sir William Sidney and widow of the second Earl of Sussex. By 1596, when the building of the new college was begun, everything of the old Franciscan house had been destroyed, save the Refectory. The architect of the new college was Ralph Symons, builder of the second court of St John's and of the hall of Trinity. The First Court of Sidney Sussex was originally of brick, but was largely rebuilt in the eighteenth and nineteenth centuries. The old Refectory of the Friars served for many years as a chapel, but was destroyed and replaced by a building designed by Essex in 1780. Quite recently the Chapel has been enlarged, and it is now one of the most interesting pieces of modern architecture in Cambridge. It is wholly Renaissance in character; the walls are panelled in oak, which displays a profusion of carving; the pavement is of elaborate marble, and the whole building has a remarkable and, perhaps, a slightly un-English individuality.

Of the college career of the greatest of the alumni of Sidney—Oliver Cromwell—very little is known. He was entered as a fellow-commoner on the day of Shakespeare's death, 23rd April 1616. He is said to have been

" more famous for his exercises in the fields than in the Schools, being one of the chief . . . players at football, cudgels, or any other boisterous sport or game," and at the end of a year's residence was obliged to leave Cambridge owing to the death of his father. When he came back to Cambridge in 1640, he was dressed " in a scarlet coat with a broad gold lace," and was shortly afterwards elected Member of Parliament for the Borough.

The famous portrait of Cromwell, which hangs in the Hall, was received by William Elliston, Master of the College, in January 1766. It was accompanied by a note stating that "an Englishman, an Assertor of Liberty, Citizen of the World," wished to present an original portrait, drawn by Cooper, to the college, and requesting that it should be placed " so as to receive the Light from Left to Right ; and to be free from Sunshine." The giver was afterwards identified with Thomas Hollis, an ardent Republican of the eighteenth century. Whether Thomas Hollis was right in assigning the portrait to Cooper is not quite certain. What is certain is that popular tradition prefers to associate it with Horace Walpole's famous anecdote of Cromwell's instructions to Sir Peter Lely :

" Mr Lely, I desire you would use all your skill to paint my picture truly like me, and not flatter me at all ; but remark all these roughnesses, pimples, warts, and everything as you see me, otherwise I never will pay a farthing for it."

Past Sidney Sussex the narrow street (now Sidney Street, but originally called Conduit Street in commemoration of the conduit for which the Franciscans were responsible) winds its way past Holy Trinity Church, where Simeon won his triumphs, up to the entrance-gateway of Christ's

College, the earlier of the two foundations of the Lady Margaret.

Like its sister-college, St John's, Christ's stands on the site of an earlier foundation—God's House, founded in connection with Clare in 1436, and removed by Henry VI from its original position to a site in Preachers' Street, just outside the town gates. The Lady Margaret obtained a charter for her new college in 1505. The principal court was begun in her lifetime, and Fuller has preserved a pleasant anecdote :

" Once the Lady Margaret came to Christ's College to behold it when partly built, and looking out of a window, saw the dean call a faulty scholar to correction ; to whom she said, ' *lente, lente*,' gently, gently, as accounting it better to mitigate his punishment than procure his pardon ; mercy and justice making the best medley to offenders."

On the gateway may be seen the Beaufort antelopes, the portcullis, the marguerites, and other heraldic emblems displayed at St John's. Unfortunately the original brick-work of the court was alternated with clunch, and the walls became so dilapidated in the eighteenth century that it was necessary for the whole of the street front, and also of the interior of the court, to be re-faced. Like the corresponding courts of Queens' and St John's, the First Court of Christ's contains all the component parts of a college. Originally the upper part of the Master's lodging was reserved for the Foundress ; and one of the rooms in the Lodge is known as " The Prayer-Room," and may have been a private oratory for the use of the Foundress and of Bishop Fisher. In the seventeenth century, further accommodation was urgently needed for the students, many of whom " lodged in ye Brazen George," on the other side of the street, and in 1642 the Fellows' Buildings were built. John Evelyn, passing through Cambridge in August 1654, described Christ's as " a very noble erection, especially the modern part, built without the quadrangle towards the gardens, of exact architecture." One set of rooms in this building contains some of the best panelling in Cambridge.

Perhaps the gardens of Christ's are more famous than its buildings, and chiefly because, as Dyer says:

" Travellers are here shewn a rich mulberry tree broken down with age, but not deserted, it being propt up with wonderful assiduity and skill, and not merely consecrated to Milton, but planted, we are told, with his own hand. Whether true or not, the fancy may be improved by supposing that Milton here meditated some of his juvenile poems, many of them, particularly his Latin Elegies, having been written by him while a student of this college, and relating to Cambridge."

What was told to travellers more than a hundred years ago is still told to-day, but the Higher Critics of Cantabrigian history assert that " Milton's Mulberry-tree " is probably the last of a number of such trees bought in 1609. Milton was admitted to Christ's in 1625, and, according to Aubrey's gossip, suffered the indignity of being flogged for some breach of college discipline. This, again, is probably apocryphal, though flogging was not unknown as an undergraduate punishment in the seventeenth century. In later years Milton wrote, " with all grateful mind," of " that more than ordinary respect which I found, above many of my equals, at the hands of those courteous and learned men, the Fellows of that college wherein I spent some years ; who, at my parting after I had taken two degrees, as the manner is, signified many ways how much better it would content them that I would stay. . . ."

Milton left Cambridge, after taking his M.A. degree, in 1632. Of the poems of Milton which are associated with Cambridge, the most famous, of course, is *Lycidas*. Edward

King, who had been admitted to Christ's in 1626, became a Fellow in 1630, and was drowned seven years later in the Irish Seas. *Lycidas* was one of a volume of poems, " ab Amicis mœrentibus," printed at the University Press in 1638, and there may be seen at the University Library a copy containing corrections in Milton's own hand.

Poems which belong more strictly to Milton's Cambridge period are *On the Morning of Christ's Nativity*, and *On Shakespear*, which was printed in the Second Folio in 1632. More popular were two poems on Thomas Hobson, the University Carrier :

> " Here lies old *Hobson*, Death hath broke his girt,
> And here alas, hath laid him in the dirt,
> Or els the ways being foul, twenty to one,
> He's here stuck in a slough, and overthrown.
> 'Twas such a shifter, that if truth were known,
> Death was half glad when he had got him down ;
> For he had any time this ten yeers full,
> Dodg'd with him, betwixt *Cambridge* and the Bull . . ."

One of the greatest of the Cambridge writers of light verse was a Christ's man—Charles Stuart Calverley, formerly Blayds of Balliol, who came to Cambridge in 1852. Amongst his contemporaries at Christ's were Walter Besant and J. R. Seeley. Calverley became a Fellow, and made the following note on a College meeting :

" *Remarked by the Master.* That no people give you so much trouble, if you try to extract money from them, as solicitors.

By the Jun. Dean. Except, perhaps, parsons.

By the Senior Dean. The latter possibly because they have not got the money.

By Mr A. That a ton weight is a great deal of books.

By Mr B. That it is just one o'clock.

By Mr C. That that is likely, and that in an hour it will be just two."

Better known to undergraduates are such poems of Calverley's as the *Ode to Tobacco* :

> " Cats may have had their goose
> Cooked by tobacco-juice ;
> Still why deny its use
>   Thoughtfully taken ?
>
> " We're not as tabbies are :
> Smith, take a fresh cigar !
> Jones, the tobacco jar !
>   Here's to thee, Bacon ! "

Even the poems of Milton and Calverley cannot have been read so regularly by freshmen as was the work of another Christ's man, William Paley, whose *Evidences of Christianity* appeared in 1794, and was, until a few years ago, a compulsory subject for " Little-go," the first Cambridge examination. Enterprising crammers produced remarkable tabular summaries of Paley's arguments for the benefit of their slower pupils, and the last Paley examination paper is carefully preserved in Christ's.

Christ's also produced the best social historian of Cambridge in the eighteenth and early nineteenth centuries—Henry Gunning, who came up in 1784 :

" The number of admissions at Christ's in my year was only three : two of the men professed not to read and I was ignorant of the first Proposition in Euclid."

There follows a picture of the college—the hasty lectures after chapel, the lecturer's gown imperfectly concealing boots and spurs ; the sudden appearance in college of two men on horseback who galloped round the court, one of a series of similar displays in various colleges undertaken for a wager by a Trinity undergraduate and a Fellow of St Catharine's ; the Junior Tutor, who hated the Master, and referred in a lecture to his " most filthy and disgusting " habit of chewing tobacco ; the undergraduate suppers with whist for shilling points and occasionally half-a-crown on the rubber; the adventure of Thomas Kipling, Doctor of Divinity, with Miss Jemima Watson; the shooting on Coe Fen, which "abounded with snipes"; the convivial entertainment given by Hare Townsend to the undergraduates of Magdalene, "whose temperate habits and devotion to tea were quite proverbial. . . ."

Gunning was sixth wrangler in 1788 and held the post of Esquire Bedell from 1789 to 1854; his *Reminiscences* form one of the most valuable of University records.

In the early nineteenth century Christ's had a very popular tutor in Jos. Shaw. He was generally to be found at Newmarket on race-days, and many of his pupils followed him. One of them was Charles Darwin, who was admitted to Christ's in 1827, and, in his own words, "got into a sporting set":

"We used often to dine together in the evening . . . and we sometimes drank too much, with jolly singing and playing at cards afterwards. I know that I ought to feel ashamed of days and evenings thus spent, but as some of my friends were very pleasant, and we were all in the highest spirits, I cannot help looking back to these times with much pleasure."

Darwin also acquired a taste for music at Cambridge, and, though he declared that he was "utterly destitute of an ear," he derived such pleasure from the anthems in King's College Chapel that his backbone would sometimes shiver; his greatest enthusiasm, however, was reserved for the collecting of beetles. In 1909 the centenary of his birth was celebrated by one of the most remarkable gatherings of men of science ever seen in Cambridge.

EMMANUEL COLLEGE: THE CHAPEL AND GALLERY

EMMANUEL COLLEGE—DOWNING COLLEGE

"SIR WALTER," said Queen Elizabeth, " I hear you have erected a puritan foundation." "No, madam," replied Sir Walter Mildmay, " far be it from me to countenance any thing contrary to your established laws ; but I have set an acorn, which, when it becomes an oak, God alone knows what will be the fruit thereof."

The acorn was Emmanuel College, founded by Sir Walter Mildmay, of Christ's in 1584, on the site previously occupied by a house of the Dominican Friars, who gave their name to the street in which their house once stood—Preachers' Street, now St Andrews' Street.

The old Dominican house was reconstructed by Ralph Symons, the church being converted into a hall, and a new chapel (now the library) being built to run north and south on the site of what may have been the friars' refectory. It is generally conjectured that the position of the chapel and the treatment of the old church were meant to emphasise the Puritan principles of the new foundation.

Opposite the Hall, and forming the south side of what is now the First Court, a long range of chambers was built, but this was entirely reconstructed in the eighteenth century. The range, however, which was built of brick some fifty years later to the south of the First Court, still remains as one of the best mellowed portions of the college fabric. Of the old chapel many complaints were made early in the seventeenth century : the building, which had never been consecrated, was falling into ruin, and the conduct of the Communion Service was lax and disorderly. Accordingly, after the end of the Civil War, William Sancroft, Master of the College from 1662 to 1665, secured the services of Christopher Wren, who was then engaged upon the chapel at Pembroke, for the building of a new chapel, which was placed in a position similar to that of Peterhouse Chapel, at the end of the First Court. Cloisters joined it with each side of the court, and above the cloisters was built a picture gallery attached to the Master's Lodge. Thanks to Wren, the view of the façade, which the traveller sees as he stands beneath the gateway of Emmanuel, is one of the most satisfying to be found in Cambridge. About the range of buildings, which faces the street, and was built by James Essex in 1775, he may be less enthusiastic. North of the college, and on the other side of Emmanuel Street, is one of the best of modern collegiate buildings—a court with one side open to the street, a cloister, and an oval sunk grass plot. A subway under Emmanuel Street joins the North Court with the old part of the college.

The property conveyed to Sir Walter Mildmay included " orchards, gardens, pondes . . . and waters " as well as the actual buildings of the Dominicans, and the gardens, " diversified by many plants, a bathing-house, bowling-green, and piece of water," are still an outstanding feature of the college.

Laurence Chaderton, the first Master, was well fitted to carry out the founder's design that Emmanuel should be a " seed-plot of learned men for the supply of the Church." The accounts of the effects of his preaching are similar to the records of the sermons of Dr Donne :

" Having once preached for two hours, he [Chaderton]

said that he had tired his hearers' patience and would leave off ; upon which the whole congregation cried out : ' For God's sake, sir, go on ! we beg you, go on ! ' . . ."

When King James I visited Cambridge in 1615, Emmanuel lived up to its tradition.   Other colleges

" were new be-painted,
Their founders eke were new be-sainted . . .
But the pure house of Emmanuel
Would not be like proud Jesabel
Nor shew her self before the king
As hypocrite, or painted thing
But, that the ways might all prove fair,
Conceiv'd a tedious mile of prayer."

One of the most famous Emmanuel names of the seventeenth century is that of John Harvard, who, in the words of an inscription on a brass tablet in the college chapel, presented by Harvard men in 1904, " emigrated to Massachusetts Bay and there dying in 1638 bequeathed to a college newly established by the General Court his library and one half of his estate ; wherefore his name is borne by Harvard College, that eldest of the seminaries which advance learning and perpetuate it to posterity throughout America."

From Emmanuel, too, came most of the members of that famous group of theologians, who were known as the Cambridge Platonists, men of learning who sought for a wider philosophy of religion than was supplied by the conventional Puritanism of the period.   Chief among them was Benjamin Whichcote, afterwards Provost of King's ; other members of the group were Ralph Cudworth, author of *The True Intellectual System of the Universe*, and Nathaniel Culverwell, who, in his *Discourse of the Light of Nature*, boldly argued that " Reason and Faith may kiss each other."

Cudworth had among his pupils William Temple, who came up as a fellow-commoner in 1644.   According to

Macaulay he " forgot at Emmanuel all the little Greek which he had brought from Bishop-Stortford," and so was ill-equipped in the famous Phalaris controversy, especially with Bentley as an antagonist. In later years Swift became his secretary, and it is conjectured that this may account for Lemuel Gulliver also being sent to Emmanuel.

William Law, author of *A Serious Call to a Devout and Holy Life*, entered Emmanuel in 1705, and was elected a fellow in 1711. Two years later he was deprived of his degrees on account of the Jacobite tendencies of his " tripos speech," and, on the accession of George I, he forfeited his fellowship by refusing to take the oath of allegiance.

Eighteenth-century university life is well illustrated in the career of Richard Farmer, who became Tutor of Emmanuel in 1767 and Master in 1775. His *Essay on the Learning of Shakespeare* had established his reputation for critical learning, and it was he who lured Dr Johnson to Cambridge, and promised him " an habitation in Emmanuel." Johnson preferred Fleet Street, but paid a high tribute to Farmer's *Essay* :

" Dr Farmer," he said, " you have done that which never was done before ; that is, you have completely finished a controversy beyond all further doubt."

Farmer was no mere arm-chair commentator. When Shakespeare was being played at the time of Stourbridge Fair, he, with his friends George Steevens, Isaac Reed, Malone, and others, used to sit every night in a specially reserved part of the pit known as " The Critics' Row." " They seemed," says Gunning, " to enjoy the play as much as the youngest persons present. . . . When the perform-ance was over, they returned on foot, and adjourned to *Emmanuel Parlour*."

Farmer held the curacy of Swavesey at the same time

as his Mastership. He "made a point of attending in all weathers" at Swavesey for the Sunday services, and after a "plain, practical sermon," he had a mutton chop at the public-house. Then his churchwarden and some farmers would visit him, and he would invariably remark, "I am going to read prayers, but shall be back by the time you have made the punch." At six o'clock he returned to Cambridge, slept in his elbow-chair until his bedmaker roused him at nine, "when, resuming his wig, he started for the *Parlour*, where the fellows were in the habit of assembling on a Sunday evening."

Not a little of the charm of eighteenth-century Cambridge is preserved in the records of the Parlour of Emmanuel.

Across the road, and a little farther to the south, are the gates of Downing College, a college which has been described, by an Oxford man, as "standing apart from 'the sights' of Cambridge and possessing neither antiquarian nor architectural interest . . . probably neglected even by the most conscientious of our foreign visitors." But the discerning visitor will certainly not neglect Downing. Founded under the will of Sir George Downing, Bart., of Gamlingay, who died in 1749, the college came into existence only after years of litigation. But in 1800 a royal charter was obtained, and four years later the site, then known as Pembroke Leys, was eventually purchased. Designs for the college buildings were submitted by several architects, and the plans of William Wilkins, who afterwards designed the New Court of Corpus, were at length accepted. The work was begun in 1807, and, according to a contemporary account, it was evident to everyone that the intention was to make a most magnificent building: "It will consist of one large stone-faced quadrangle, more spacious than that of Trinity College; the south side will be 500 feet long. It will be composed of the Keton stone. The master's lodge is an elegant specimen of the Ionic order : the entrance of the college will be of the Doric ; and these two orders will run through the whole quadrangle."

But of this great quadrangle only two sides, the east and west, were completed. At the time of their erection, architectural opinion rated them highly ; later in the century the wave of Gothic enthusiasm swamped any appreciation of buildings which could show neither pinnacles nor pointed arches nor vaulted roofs ; to-day, though most people will probably agree with Maria Edgeworth in thinking that Downing "will never bear comparison with King's College Chapel," there is a saner appreciation of the beautiful stone and the quiet dignity of the Downing buildings. In the later part of the nineteenth century financial troubles compelled the college to sell some portions of its grounds ; and, though its domain still has an appearance of spaciousness, it is blocked at one end by the houses of Lensfield Road and at the other by the constantly-growing mass of university laboratories.

The charter of the college ordained that the foundation should include a Professor of the Laws of England and a Professor of Medicine. The first occupant of the Chair of Medicine was Sir Busick Harwood, of whom Gunning has much to say in his *Reminiscences* ; of the Law professors, one of the greatest was Frederick William Maitland, who held the post from 1888 to 1906. His successor, Courtney Stanhope Kenny, is remembered not only for his wide and genial learning, but also for the quality of his legal text-books. His name is commemorated in the new gates leading into Tennis Court Road.

But the greatest Downing "character" of the nineteenth

century was John Perkins, a contemporary of Calverley at Christ's, who became a Fellow of Downing in 1861. He combined his various college offices with the secretaryship of the Cambridgeshire Hunt for many years, and appeared in *Vanity Fair* in " pink " with the single word " Downing " beneath.

In 1932 there was completed a portion of the new range of buildings, designed by Sir Herbert Baker and built in Ketton stone, on the north side of the quadrangle. The chapel and library remain to be built and Downing will be the first college in Cambridge to boast of a dome.

EPILOGUE

EPILOGUE

SO from Peterhouse to Downing, from the end of the
thirteenth to the beginning of the nineteenth century
the development of university life may be traced in the
constituent colleges. In the nineteenth century new colleges
and kindred institutions have been established. Selwyn
College was founded in memory of Bishop George Augustus
Selwyn in 1882 as " a College wherein sober living and high
culture of the mind may be combined with Christian training,
based upon the principles of the Church of England," and has
grown and flourished since the time of its foundation.

Of the two women's colleges, Girton stands in rural
isolation on the Huntingdon Road, Newnham is nearer to the
heart of the town. Women students are still denied full
membership of the university, but, after many years of
controversy, they have won their titular degrees, and, in
practice, every academic avenue, except that which leads to
the Senate House, is now open to them. Perhaps the two
most important features of modern Cambridge are the in-
creases in the numbers of undergraduates and in the numbers
of subjects which they may study. Until the middle of the
nineteenth century there were but two honours examinations—the mathematical and the classical tripos. Now there
are fourteen triposes as well as a bewildering series of com-
binations of subjects by which a pass degree may be
obtained. Moreover, the development of each new branch

of science demands not only a new examination, but a new laboratory.

The colleges are similarly pressed for room, and, in spite of their new buildings, are compelled to hire lodgings for a certain proportion of their undergraduates. Few college halls are large enough for all the members to dine at one sitting.

Yet, although a member of the older Cambridge may return, like Dr Caius, to find a "marvellous transformation," though he may deplore motor-cars and tea-shops and hot baths and the new pronunciation of Latin and the English Tripos and the abolition of compulsory Greek and voluntary attendance at chapel and a hundred other symptoms of decadence, he will find, nevertheless, that the essential features of college life persist through every phase of administrative and material change. The American visitor who expressed surprise at "finding the old ruins inhabited," was a better commentator than he knew. College buildings are not merely monuments of the piety or grandeur of the past; they are still the dwelling-places of youth. In the continuity of college fabric and tradition lies the greatest of the charms of Cambridge.

Printed in Great Britain by Lowe & Brydone (Printers), Ltd., London, N.W.1.